THOU SHALT NOT
KILL

The Christian Case against Abortion

THOU SHALT NOT KILL

KILL

Edited by RICHARD L. GANZ

ARLINGTON HOUSE·PUBLISHERS
NEW ROCHELLE, NEW YORK

261.8
Tho

Book design by Pat Slesarchik

Manufactured in the United States of America

Chapter 1 is adapted from
The Right to Live, The Right to Die,
copyright © 1976 by Tyndale House
Publishers. Used by permission.

Library of Congress Cataloging in Publication Data

Main entry under title:
Thou shalt not kill.

1. Abortion—Religious aspects—Addresses,
essays, lectures. I. Ganz, Richard L., 1946–
HQ767.3.T48   261.8′3   78–15964
ISBN 0–87000–406–9

Contents

Foreword

For two reasons I heartily commend this book to all thinking persons—Christians and non-Christians alike. First, it is the best book about abortion that I have seen. Considered for information and argumentation as well as for breadth and depth of coverage of its subject, it is unparalleled. Here is a wealth of convincing, challenging, thought-provoking, incisive, usable material for nearly everyone who is concerned about abortion. And the style of writing (fortunately) is popular rather than technical. Yet, unlike most popular writing, the articles are far from superficial.

The authors are not sensationalists; they are all solid scholars in the fields about which they write, as the biographical notes indicate. What they say, therefore, is factual, reliable, and (I believe) definitive. All of the authors of this volume are Christians who are fully committed to the inerrant Word of God as the foundation for their thought and action. This rings out most clearly in Professor Frame's excellent exegetical study, but that it firmly undergirds the rest of the articles is apparent to those who have the eyes to see.

The second reason why I am happy to commend this book is that I know four of the contributors personally. I have worked closely with Dr. Richard Ganz at the Christian Counseling and Educational Foundation of Laverock, Pennsylvania, where I have had the opportunity to observe his excellent work firsthand. I have come to respect Rich's deep concern for people and his thorough work in helping them. What he has written here unmistakably reflects those two qualities: concern and thoroughness. Professor John Frame has been my colleague as a member of the faculty of Westminster Theological Seminary for a number of years as well as a fellow minister in the Orthodox Presbyterian Church. Over the years my appreciation for his deep fidelity to the Scriptures and his unusually precise way of putting things has grown. His lucid pen and straightforward understanding of and argumentation from the biblical data felicitously combine to make a case that is at once profound and satisfyingly simple. Professor Harold O. J. Brown is a recent acquaintance but I have long known him from afar through his books. I have encountered a remarkably unanimous consensus of highly favorable opinion about him and his work from many trustworthy witnesses. I know Mrs. Foh both personally (through Westminster Theological Seminary) and from her previous excellent work on women's questions. Her present chapter, by demolishing the feminists' major arguments, establishes her as a leading voice for the Christian position on women's lib and abortion.

You can understand the anticipation and enthusiasm with which I picked up the typed manuscript of this book. I was not disappointed. That is saying a lot because lately I have again and again become discouraged with what I have read. So many books are repetitious, frothy, eclectic, or a combination of all of these. It is a joy to commend one that has all of the opposite characteristics!

Here, then, is a book to buy, to read, to lend, and to reread carefully. It is unquestionably the best in its field.

JAY E. ADAMS
Dean, the Institute of Pastoral Studies
Editor, *The Journal of Pastoral Practice*
   of the
Christian Counseling and Education Foundation
   and
Visiting Professor of Practical Theology
Westminster Theological Seminary

1 A Physician Looks at Abortion

C. Everett Koop, M.D.

In 1959 the United Nations passed the following resolution as part of its Declaration of Human Rights: "The child, by reason of its physical and mental immaturity, needs special safeguards in care, including appropriate legal protection before as well as after birth."[1]

Then on January 22, 1973 the Supreme Court of the United States (*Roe v. Wade* and *Doe v. Bolton*) announced essentially that it had discovered a new personal liberty in the Constitution—the liberty of a woman to procure the termination of her pregnancy at any time in its course on demand.[2] The termination of a pregnancy is abortion.

Long before the Supreme Court's decision there were forces at work in the United States preparing us for the day when abortion on demand would be the law of the land. The Supreme Court went far beyond the wildest imaginations of the most ardent pro-abortionists. Over several years, by techniques of deceit and misrepresentation, by brainwashing, and by tricky use of semantics, the people of the United States were led toward acceptance of abortion on demand.

We were informed that thousands upon thousands of women had lost their lives from illegal abortions done in back rooms by shady characters when in actuality in no one year did this figure ever exceed several hundred.[3] We who as a people always knew that abortion was the killing of an unborn baby were brainwashed to believe that the destruction of the "products of conception" or the destruction of a "fetus" is not the same thing as killing an unborn baby. Traditional medical definitions were deliberately changed in order to do away with our moral repugnance toward abortion. For example, in 1965 the American College of Obstetricians and Gynecologists changed the definition of human pregnancy. Conception ceased to mean fertilization; conception began after implantation. The terms "postconceptive contraception" (doubletalk of the highest magnitude) and "postconceptive fertility control" came into being as synonyms for abortion.[4]

Although I have reasons against abortion that are theological as well as logical, I will stick to the logic of a medical presentation.

Development of the Baby in the Uterus

It is impossible for anyone to say when a developing fetus or embryo or baby becomes viable; that is, has the ability to exist on its own. The logical approach is to go back to the sperm and the egg. A sperm has 23 chromosomes, and even though it is alive and can fertilize an egg, it can never make another sperm. An egg also has 23 chromosomes and it can never make another egg. So we have eggs that cannot reproduce and we have sperm that cannot reproduce. Unless the two get together. Once sperm and egg unite, and the 23 chromosomes of each are brought together into one cell with 46 chromosomes, we have an entirely different story. That one cell with its 46 chromosomes contains the whole genetic code, written in molecules of DNA (deoxyribonucleic acid), that will, if not interrupted, make a human being just like you or me, with the potential for God-consciousness. I do not know anyone among my medical confreres, no matter how pro-abortion he might be, who would kill a newborn baby the minute he was born. (He might let him starve to death. He would not kill him.)[5] My question to my pro-abortion friend who will not kill a newborn baby is this: "Would you kill this infant a minute before he was born, or a minute before that, or a minute before that, or a minute before that?" You see what I am getting at. How can one consider life to be worthless one minute, and the next minute consider that same life to be precious? So much for logic.

. By the time a baby is 18 to 25 days old, long before the mother is sure that she is pregnant, his heart is already beating. At 45 days after conception, you can pick up electroencephalographic waves from the baby's developing brain. At eight weeks not only is there a brain, but the fingerprints on the hands have already formed and except for size will never change. By the ninth and tenth weeks, the thyroid and the adrenal glands are functioning. The baby can squint, swallow, and move his tongue. The sex hormones are already present. By 12 and 13 weeks he has fingernails, he sucks his thumb, and he can recoil from pain. In the fourth month the growing baby is eight to ten inches in height. In the fifth month there is a time of lengthening and strengthening of the developing infant. Skin, hair, and nails grow. Sweat glands arise. Oil glands excrete. This is the month in which the mother feels the movements of her infant. It has always seemed extraordinary to me that as the pregnant woman feels the first movements within her uterus, she inevitably says, "Today I felt life." In the sixth month the developing baby responds to light and sound. He sleeps and awakens. He gets hiccups and can hear the beat of his mother's heart. Survival outside the womb is now possible. In the seventh month the nervous system becomes much more complex, the infant is 16 inches long and weighs about three pounds. The final eighth and ninth months are a time of fattening and of continued growth.[6]

Techniques of Abortion

There are three commonly used techniques of abortion; each may have its variations. The technique that is used most commonly for early pregnancies is called the D & C, or dilation and curettage. In this technique, which is carried out between the seventh and twelfth weeks of pregnancy, the uterus is approached through the vagina. The cervix is stretched to permit the insertion of instruments. The surgeon then scrapes the wall of the uterus, cutting the baby's body to pieces and scraping the placenta from its attachments on the uterine wall. Bleeding is considerable.[7] An alternative method used in the same period of pregnancy is called suction abortion. The principle is the same as in D & C. More than 66 percent of all abortions performed in the United States and Canada are done by this method.[8] A powerful suction tube is inserted through the open cervix. This tears apart the body of the developing baby and his placenta, sucking them into a jar. These smaller parts of the body are recognizable as arms, legs, head, etc.

Later in pregnancy, when the D & C or suction abortion

might produce too great a hemorrhage from the mother, the second most common type of abortion comes into play. This is called the salt-poisoning abortion, or "salting out." After 16 weeks of pregnancy, when enough fluid has accumulated in the sac around the baby, a rather long needle is inserted through the mother's abdomen directly into the sac surrounding the baby and a solution of concentrated salt is injected into it. The baby breathes in and swallows the salt. It poisons him. The outer layer of the baby's skin is burned off by the high concentration of the salt. The osmotic pressure changes; brain hemorrhages are frequent. It takes about an hour slowly to kill the baby by this method. The mother usually goes into labor about a day later and delivers a dead, shriveled baby.[9]

If abortion is decided upon too late for the D & C or salting-out procedures, there is left a final technique of abortion called hysterotomy. A hysterotomy is exactly the same as a cesarean section, with the one difference, namely, that in a cesarean section the operation is done to save the life of the baby whereas in the hysterotomy it is done to kill the baby.[10] These babies look very much like other babies except that they are small, weighing, for example, about two pounds at the end of a 24-week pregnancy. Though truly alive, they are allowed to die through neglect or are deliberately killed by a variety of methods.

Hysterotomy gives the fetus the best chance, but at a very high price in morbidity and at a risk of mortality for the mother 15 times greater than that of saline infusion, the more commonly used alternative.[11] A Boston jury found a physician guilty of manslaughter for killing the product of this type of abortion.[12]*In a second major blow to the unborn child, the Supreme Court on July 1, 1976 essentially gave the physician the right to do whatever the family wishes with the baby after hysterotomy.[13] So in a very brief period of time we made an act that was considered manslaughter into nothing more than a medical decision. As a matter of fact, the baby in this instance

*In New York City in 1957–59, 28-week live-born infants had a 60 percent probability of survival. In 1966–70 in Montreal such infants had a 92.2 percent chance of surviving the first week after birth. The 1973 maternal death rate for amniotic-fluid exchange (saline abortion) was 19 per 100,000. The 1973 maternal death rate for hysterotomy abortion was 79.9 per 100,000.[14]

11

does not even enjoy the same protocol as would a tumor removed from the same uterus.

That children can be born alive in abortions performed by hysterotomy is a fact. In *Markle v. Able,* a case decided by the Supreme Court of the United States,[15] a table appears listing 27 live births after abortions; there have been many more. Babies delivered by hysterotomy with the intent of abortion are obviously a source of concern to abortionists. In the collected letters of the International Correspondence Society of Obstetricians and Gynecologists (November 1, 1974), the question was how obstetricians handle live births that occur during abortions. A Philadelphia physician wrote: "At the time of delivery it has been our policy to wrap the fetus in a towel. The fetus is then moved to another room, while our attention is turned to the care of the gravida [former mother-to-be]. She is examined to determine whether placental expulsion has occurred and the extent of vaginal bleeding. Once we are sure her condition is stable, the fetus is evaluated. Almost invariably all signs of *life* have ceased"[16] (emphasis added).

Consequences of Abortion

It is very difficult to obtain statistics in this country that illuminate the effects of abortion on the woman. The 1973 Supreme Court ruling, which made possible the establishment of free-standing abortion clinics outside the scrutiny of the Joint Committee on the Accreditation of Hospitals, aids and abets the loss of statistical data for these purposes. In addition there is almost a conspiracy of silence about the results of abortion. Presumably this is to make it difficult for the anti-abortion forces to buttress their position with valid statistics. In the years 1974, 1975, and 1976, for instance, two of the leading journals of obstetrics and gynecology in the United States published 34 articles dealing with the problems of prostaglandin-induced abortions that gave no statistics on the number of live-born infants. When an infant is live-born after a prostaglandin-induced abortion this really is a complication. All of the other side effects of the drug were well documented except the production of living children.[17]

Experience in Other Countries

In other countries that have gone the way of abortion on demand, there have been developments from which we can learn. Japan is one of these countries. It liberalized abortions just about the way we did, but in 1948. The first year there were 250,000 abortions[18]; in the first eight years Japanese women had 5,000,000 abortions. The Japanese experience indicates that as people became used to abortion—as it ceased to be a shocking thing to talk about, and as people talked about products of conception rather than about unborn babies—abortions took place later and later in pregnancy. By 1956, 26,000 abortions in Japan were at five months, 20,000 were at six months, and 7,000 were at seven months.[19] In 1972 there were no fewer than 1,500,000 abortions. Dr. T. A. Ueno, professor at Nihan University in Tokyo, concluded: "We can now say that the law is a bad one." He remarked to the International Academy of Legal and Social Medicine, meeting in Rome: "The sooner Japan returns to a solid law which forbids the taking of the life of the unborn, the better for our nation."[20] Poland enacted a liberal abortion law many years ago, but recently the government reversed itself. So many Polish women were having abortions that the birth rate had fallen well below the "population zero" level. Poland was committing genocide—against itself. We are doing the same thing.

The National Health Service in Great Britain keeps excellent records, and it has been in the abortion-on-demand business for about eight years. The pro-abortionists in this country, in the days before the Supreme Court's decision, told us how legalized abortion would curb illegitimacy, prostitution, venereal disease, and other social ills. Unfortunately, the excellent records of the first five years of liberalized abortion under the National Health Service in Great Britain have revealed an increase in illegitimacy, venereal disease, prostitution, and in pelvic inflammatory disease from gonorrhea, as well as in sterility of previously aborted mothers and subsequent spontaneous abortions or miscarriages. Ectopic pregnancies—where the egg is fertilized not in the uterus but up in the fallopian tube, requiring an emergency abdominal operation—have doubled since abortion has been liberalized. Prematurity in British women who have had a previous abortion is 40 percent higher than in those who have not.[21] No one has done a study of the emotional reaction or the guilt of the woman who has had an abortion and now desperately wants a baby she cannot have.

In May 1976 the *British Medical Journal* reported a paper by Richardson and Dixon entitled "The Effects of Legal Termination on Subsequent Pregnancy."[22] The study was carried out on 211 patients who had undergone a vaginal abortion and were pregnant again. Of these 211 patients, 43.2 percent had become pregnant within one year of the abortion. The overall fetal loss in the 211 patients was 17.5 percent, compared with only 7.5 percent in a controlled group matched for number of previous pregnancies but consisting of patients who were pregnant after a *spontaneous* abortion (miscarriage). All together, 4.3 percent of the pregnancies after legal abortion ended as first-trimester abortions, 8.5 percent as second-trimester abortions, 13.7 percent in premature delivery. Among 11 women whose cervices had been lacerated at the time of the abortion, the fetal loss in subsequent pregnancy was 45.5 percent and only one pregnancy went beyond 36 weeks.

An especially interesting aspect of the study was that several patients had asked that their family doctor not be told of the previous abortion; such patients might have been helped had the practitioner known about the defective cervix. There was no evidence to indicate that the infants of patients with the history of a previous abortion were small for their date of delivery. It is also interesting that there were nine deaths among the 29 newborns delivered prematurely in the abortion group. None of these was due to a fetal abnormality. Several other infants were being followed by their pediatricians, who expected a high morbidity or delayed mortality in this group. Indeed, two infants had already died in early infancy. Finally, the social grounds on which the request for abortion had been mainly based often remained unchanged at the beginning of the subsequent pregnancy.

A research analyst, Barbara J. Syska, has done a study on what the results of the Richardson and Dixon statistics might mean for the one million American women who aborted their babies last year.[23] Projecting from such a small sample gives only a rough estimate, but close enough to reveal the magnitude of the problems produced by abortion. About 430,000 women who had abortions would not now be pregnant a second time had they carried their babies to term, since there would

14

be no time for them to get pregnant. (Only a very small percentage of women are physically able to get pregnant within three months after their baby is born.) Inasmuch as 47.8 percent of all abortions are abortions performed on women who have no living children,[24] Syska had this to say about the 478,000 women of the preceding million who aborted their first babies: "As many as 88,000 will lose their 'wanted' baby. Taking into account the normal infant mortality in the United States for 1974 (16.7 per 1,000), 26,000 infants would die solely because their mothers had abortions beforehand. It is also possible that had it not been for abortion the infant mortality could go from 16.7 per 100,000 live births to 8.4 per 100,000 live births." In 1974 there were 52,776 infant deaths in the United States.

Alfred Kotasek is a medical doctor and professor-in-charge of the Department of Gynecology and Obstetrics, Charles University, Prague, Czechoslovakia. The paper he originally presented to the fourth International Congress on Perinatal Medicine in Prague in January 1975 has been printed as a report from Czechoslovakia in the *Human Life Review*.[25] It is important to know that Kotasek is not against abortion per se; he is opposed to family planning by abortion. Kotasek starts off by indicating that legalized abortion has cut down on the back-street element in many countries of the world, but nevertheless many of the bad consequences remain. He makes it very clear that the prevalence of postabortion morbidity reported by many writers from different countries depends upon *how long* the women concerned were kept under surveillance after the abortion. The longer the surveillance, the higher the morbidity reported. To quote Kotasek: "No wonder that early complications are found in about 5 to 10 percent of women, whereas permanent or 'longer term' complications are recorded in 15, 30, 50, or even 70 percent of all women who undergo abortions."

Abortion in Czechoslovakia on social (i.e., nonmedical) grounds is not permitted if the period of gestation exceeds 12 weeks. The experience there covers nearly 2,000,000 legal first-trimester abortions over a period of 17 years. In contrast, complications from midtrimester abortions are reported primarily from other countries. The morbidity resulting from legal abortions seems to be directly related to the type of procedure undertaken.

Kotasek sums up his findings on morbidity and mortality as follows:

MORBIDITY AND MORTALITY FOLLOWING LEGAL
ABORTION

I. First-trimester abortions
  A. Immediate complications
    Death following induced abortion
    Excessive blood loss
    Injuries to the cervix
    Perforation of the uterus

  B. Early complications
    Fever
    Bleeding
    Retained products of conception
    Infection of endometrium and myometrium
    "Postabortal pain syndrome"

  C. "Long-term" complications
    Chronic inflammatory conditions of the genital organs,
    latent inflammatory conditions of the genital organs
    Menstrual disorders
    Psychological and psychiatric complications
    Disorders of sexual life and behavior
    Sterility

  D. Latent morbidity apparent during a subsequent pregnancy
    Extrauterine pregnancy
    Isoimmunization (Rh, ABO)
    Spontaneous abortions; midtrimester abortions (cervical
    incompetence)
    Increase in perinatal mortality (stillbirths)
    Increase in premature births
    Greater frequency of hemorrhage during pregnancy
    Longer average duration of labor
    Retained and adherent placentae
    Severe hemorrhage at parturition

Kotasek goes on to document and describe in detail each of
these complications from the world literature.

It was clear from all of the studies that there was a high

incidence of spontaneous abortions (miscarriages) resulting from previous abortion. A detailed study from Prague concluded that only 57 percent of pregnancies following an abortion resulted in a term delivery; the miscarriage rate was 2.2 times higher than normal. In another Prague study infertility occurred in 20 percent of patients who had had an abortion. There was a tenfold increase in second-trimester miscarriages in pregnancies that followed an induced abortion, most of these explained by cervical incompetence.

Kotasek's report showed that a very high standard of antenatal care was necessary from the end of the first trimester for all women who had had a previous abortion. If the abortion had been a midtrimester abortion, the cervix had to be examined every week or at least every two weeks. The unfortunate thing learned from this study is that abortion affects not only the mother, but any "wanted" baby she may subsequently bear. Preliminary data on a series of 63 subjects with an incompetent cervix indicated that approximately 30 percent of the surviving infants born of these pregnancies had abnormal neurological findings at the age of one year.

There was a higher incidence of prematurity, the percentage of stillbirths jumped, the third stage of labor (expulsion of the placenta) became significantly longer, and retained or adherent placentae were more common after a previous induced abortion. All of these findings in the Czechoslovakian study, supported by Evans and Ellsworth, dealt with first-trimester (13 weeks) abortions.

Complications from abortion in the midtrimester are considered to be three or four times more likely than in early abortion. There are possible complications to the mother from the intraamniotic injection of hypertonic salt solution, as well as a number of postabortal complications. A saline injection takes 33 hours, plus or minus 13 hours, to induce an abortion. When the abortion time following salting-out was longer than 22 hours, excessive bleeding was almost three times as common and retained placenta was more than four times as common. In a number of instances the dead baby was reportedly pushed out through a posterior ureterovaginal fistula, bypassing the undilated cervix after the intraamniotic injection of saline solution.

Kotasek concludes that abortion increases the risk of subsequent spontaneous abortions (miscarriages); midterm abortions, especially, may result in latent cervical incompetence, which increases the proportion of premature births and ectopic pregnancies, and produces a number of complications affecting subsequent pregnancies. In addition, abortion frequently reduces a woman's future reproductive capability and affects her emotional and sexual life. Abortion cannot be regarded as a safe and simple contraceptive method, Kotasek says, although he would allow it as a backup to be used when family planning fails. (Remember that Kotasek has no moral scruples against abortion.)

Kotasek also concludes that since late abortion is three to four times more risky than early abortion, pregnancies to be aborted on social grounds should be terminated before the 13th week. Abortion must never be allowed to replace adequate preventive care, which he defines as sex education in school and education for planned and conscientious parenthood.

Abortion in the United States

Although a number of articles having to do with abortion have been published in scientific journals in the United States, not many of them deal with the complications of abortion, especially the long-term complications. No psychiatric study of the aborted mother's guilt feelings has been done. As I mentioned earlier, statistics in the United States are hard to come by because the free-standing abortion clinics do not report to the Joint Committee on the Accreditation of Hospitals. It is reasonable to assume that when medical centers associated with medical schools publish their findings, the data will be more reliable than those collected in free-standing abortion clinics. But even in the latter instance it is obvious from some studies available that legal abortion is still a loathsome thing to many women who seek one.

Matthew Bulfin has done a study on more than 300 patients who previously had legal abortions and then saw him as a gynecologist.[26] He developed a set of questions that he asked this selected group of patients. Here are some of the things he learned.

The vast majority of women would not have had an abortion if it were illegal to do so. This would seem to indicate that they equated legality with what was "right" and with the safety of the procedure.

For 90 percent of the women, a physician apparently never entered into the decision to have an abortion. Interestingly enough, most of the patients never consulted a doctor; the patient made the decision herself in collaboration with a boyfriend or a husband or a girlfriend. Most fascinating of all is that the majority of the women did not even know the name of the doctor who performed the abortion, something that seems to nibble away at the foundations of that remarkable right that the Supreme Court has so emphasized—the right of privacy that exists between the woman and her physician.

The great majority of patients did not seem to recall any discussion of the risks of the abortion itself or the possible risks to future childbearing. Most did not recall that hemorrhages, uterine perforations, pelvic abscesses, or infection was mentioned. Many said that the clinic's physician seemed to be more interested in having all the legal releases signed and in getting paid.

Not one patient ever admitted to having any kind of thorough examination until the actual pelvic examination that was done as the abortion was about to be started. Urine tests apparently were common.

Did the husband or boyfriend of the pregnant woman know about the coming abortion? It was obvious that the woman frequently procured the abortion without the knowledge of her spouse because she gave an incorrect name and address. Boyfriends seemed to know more about abortions than husbands, probably because the boyfriend was often paying the doctor's bill.

In response to the part of the questionnaire that asked about complications after the abortion for which a physician had to be called, many patients acknowledged hemorrhage and pain. About 30 percent of the patients needed medical attention after the abortion. One patient had been hospitalized for six weeks after extensive uterine and bowel damage requiring an abdominal operation with uterine repair and a colostomy. Not surprisingly, she suffered a severe depression afterward and required psychiatric care. Many patients were hospitalized for sepsis, pelvic abscesses, and loss of blood. When the first problems of complication occurred, did the patient call the physician who did the abortion? Most women reported that they did not know the name of the doctor or had no confidence in him and therefore usually called their own gynecologist or went to the emergency room of the nearest hospital. Most did not even report their complications; they wanted "nothing more to do" with "that doctor." One question asked the women who returned to the clinic that did the abortion what kind of postoperative care they received. Here are some of the answers: "The nurse examined me and gave me some birth control pills." "I never saw any doctor." "I called the clinic but the doctor who did my abortion was only there on Tuesday mornings." "I called the clinic but got an answering service. I was told to call my own doctor if I had any problems because the clinic was closed on weekends."

When asked what they remembered most vividly about the abortion experience, the women gave some interesting answers: "The noise of the suction machine." "The relief when it was over." "The complete indifference of the doctor." "The sad faces of the other girls in the waiting room." "The pain." "Worrying that my mom and dad might find out." "My boyfriend would not even come with me."

Dr. Bulfin no longer asks this question, although he did in the beginning: "Were you aware at any time that you might be destroying a human life when you had your abortion?" The reason he has stopped asking this question is that too many patients either broke down in tears or became upset because they thought he might be about to impose a religious prejudice on them. Incidentally, it is Dr. Bulfin's routine with his pregnant women to have the mother-to-be listen to the baby's heartbeat with a stethoscope. His observation is that once a patient hears her baby's heartbeat, she seldom wants an abortion.

Amniocentesis

Amniocentesis is a medical test in which a needle is inserted directly into the pregnant woman's amniotic fluid (bag of waters) and some of the fluid extracted. It is then possible to examine a sample of the cells in this fluid and, on the basis of chromosomal studies, to gauge the possibility that a defective baby is in the uterus. Genetic counseling used to advise contraception to prevent the birth of defective children; now genetic counseling frequently seeks out defective fetuses by amniocentesis and then recommends abortion to destroy the defective child. Whereas only a few congenital defects are now diagnosable by this technique, it is quite possible that in days ahead prenatal diagnosis will be able to identify nearly all defective babies.

The National Foundation for Infantile Paralysis, popularly called the March of Dimes, once had as its goal the elimination of birth defects through education and research. Now the National Foundation has established genetic counseling services that identify the defective baby by amniocentesis and then recommend that the unborn child be destroyed by abortion. It would seem that the March of Dimes has found the cause of congenital defects, namely, pregnancy. The cure is simple: eliminate the pregnancy by abortion.

Live Fetal Research

One of the byproducts of the concern over abortion is the question of fetal experimentation. Human beings in the pre-birth stages of development, no longer protected by law since the 1973 ruling of the Supreme Court regarding abortion, are now available to medical research for experimentation in far larger numbers than ever before.

It has been the custom in medical research that when a human subject is necessary to obtain information that cannot be gleaned from animal experimentations, he is informed of the dangers of the experiment and then has the privilege of consenting or refusing to go on with it. When the subject for an experiment is an adult who can understand and give informed consent, there are few ethical problems. But when the subject is an aborted fetus, permission is not possible except from the mother, who did not want the child in the first place. It is unlikely that she will come to the defense of the fetus.

It has been almost axiomatic that when human experimentation is carried out, even with informed consent, the subject of the experiment expects that something might be gleaned from the experiment for his immediate or eventual benefit. A person may not consent to acts that might constitute murder, manslaughter, or mayhem upon himself.[27]

In spite of the Bill of Rights for Children drawn up by the United Nations in November 1959, the United States Supreme Court has withdrawn legal protection from the unborn. Fetuses are aborted at various ages. Certainly if a child survives an abortion procedure, no matter what his age, he should be considered a premature baby with all the rights of any other premature baby. His "wantedness" should not determine whether one baby is experimented upon before he dies and the other is afforded the ultimate in sophisticated therapy aimed at his survival.

There is no doubt that some researchers are experimenting upon live aborted babies. Bizarre as it may seem, vivisection is being practiced on human fetuses while the same procedure on animals is widely condemned. Experiments varying from the removal of an organ (such as the liver) from a living fetus to connecting the decapitated head of a living fetus to a heart-lung machine to study the effect of chemicals on the brain are matters of medical report.[28] Experiments like these bring no benefit to the subject, in contrast to experiments such as those of Liley, who developed a technique for transfusing blood to the baby *in utero.* Dr. Liley's comment: "The unborn child is my patient and I have respect for and protect his life as I would the life of any other patient."[29]

The Supreme Court has denied the fact that the fetus *in utero,* the unborn baby, is a person. The whole specter of live fetal research is one of the byproducts of the new right of abortion on demand.

The Future

Medical research has only begun to uncover the effects of abortion. However, when a society submits to brainwashing, when a society fails to protest a change in the plain meaning of words, when a society refuses to cry out against injustice, then the roots of the family and of civilization itself are in jeopardy. The history of Germany between World War I and World War II should never be forgotten. The actions of the Nazi regime against the Jews, against clergymen, against Russian soldiers, against gypsies, and against Germans of unpopular political opinion were possible because the medical profession in Germany had laid the foundations for mass murder. Hardly anyone had protested.

Abortion was illegal in Germany but was widely practiced after World War I. The euthanasia society sprang up shortly after that. Eventually the medical profession agreed to the extermination of the aged, the retarded, the infirm, then defec-

22

tive children, then tuberculosis patients, and so on. After Germany had raised no objection to the extermination of the first 273,000 patients under the euthanasia program, it did not take much for Hitler to extend the killing to other categories of people.

In a sense one could say that the horror of Auschwitz started with abortion and euthanasia. We are on the top of the subtle, slippery slope that leads to Auschwitz. Never let it be said that it cannot happen here. Never let historians say that we failed to learn the lessons of history.

Notes

1. United Nations Declaration on the Rights of the Child, November 20, 1959, *Everyman's United Nations*, 8th Ed. (New York: United Nations, 1971), p. 360.

2. 410 U.S. 113 (1973).

3. J. R. Stanton, *Abortion: Flawed Premise and Promise*, to be published.

4. *Terminology Bulletin*, American College of Obstetricians and Gynecologists, September 1965.

5. Report of the Joseph P. Kennedy Foundation International Symposium on Human Rights, Retardation, and Research, held at the John F. Kennedy Center for the Performing Arts, Washington, D.C., October 16, 1971; *Newsweek*, November 12, 1973, p. 70.

6. L. B. Arey, *Development Anatomy: A Textbook and Laboratory Manual of Embryology*, 7th ed. (Philadelphia: W. B. Saunders, 1965), pp. 85–105.

7. L. M. Hellman and J. A. Pritchard, eds., *Williams' Obstetrics*, 14th ed. (New York: Appleton Century Crofts, 1971), pp. 1089–91.

8. R. C. Benson, *Handbook of Obstetrics and Gynecology* (Los Altos, Calif.: Lange Medical Publishers, 1974), p. 438.

9. J. M. Mackenzie, A. Roufa, H. M. Lovell, "Midtrimester Abortion: Clinical Experience with Amniocentesis and Hypertonic Instillation in 400 Patients," *Clinical Obstetrics and Gynecology*, 14 (1971), pp. 107–24.

10. J. Peel and M. Potts, "Hysterotomy," *Textbook of Contraceptive Practice* (Cambridge: Cambridge University Press, 1969), pp. 197–98.

11. P. G. Stubblefield, "Abortion vs. Manslaughter," *Surgery*, 110 (1975), p. 790

12. Stanton, *Abortion: Flawed Premise and Promise*.

13. *Planned Parenthood v. Danforth.*

14. U. S. Center for Disease Control, Atlanta, Ga., January 18, 1975.

15. *Markle v. Able,* Supreme Court of the United States, #72–56, 72–30, p. 72.

16. Newsletter of Americans United for Life, February 1975.

17. Newsletter of American Association Pro-Life Obstetricians and Gynecologists, August 1976.

18. "Birth Crisis in Japan," *South Bend Tribune,* July 26, 1974 (quoted by J. O'Meara in *Human Life Review,* 1:4 (1975).

19. *Marriage and Family Newsletter,* May-June, 1973.

20. "Birth Crisis in Japan," *loc. cit.*

21. H. Stallworthy, A. S. Moolgaokeras, and J. J. Walsh, "Legal Abortion: A Critical Assessment of Its Risks," *Lancet* (1971), pp. 1245–49.

22. J. A. Richardson and G. Dixon, "Effects of Legal Termination on Subsequent Pregnancy," *British Medical Journal,* May 29, 1976, pp. 1303–04.

23. Newsletter of National Right to Life Committee, Summer 1976.

24. *Abortion Surveillance 1974* (Atlanta: Center for Disease Control, 1976), p. 10.

25. A. Kotasek, "Medical Consequences of Induced Abortion and Its Effect on Subsequent Pregnancy," *Human Life Review,* 2:2 (1976), pp. 118–26.

26. Newsletter of Americans United for Life, February 1975.

27. *Drug Research Report,* July 25, 1973, p. 52.

28. *Washington Post,* March 15, 1973; *Medical World News,* June 18, 1973, p. 21.

29. W. R. Buckley, "The Scientific Side of Abortion," *Cincinnati Enquirer,* April 13, 1973.

2 Psychology and Abortion: The Deception Exposed

Richard L. Ganz

The psychiatric-psychological profession has greatly influenced the "progress" of abortion in this country. Much of the profession's influence can be attributed to the myth it has perpetrated on the public—the myth that its outlook is objective and its analysis of the abortion question is from a neutral position. It is the purpose of this paper to expose the fact that the psychiatric-psychological profession, in its investigations and recommendations on abortion, operates from a set of unsubstantiated presuppositions. Its position on abortion is fixed to these presuppositions and inflexible to the facts. By ignoring facts that do not fit within their philosophical framework and warping others to conform to their prefabricated structure, psychiatrists and psychologists have distorted the truth and debased the sanctity of life to suit their own definition of the nature and worth of human existence. Let us examine their presuppositions in the following areas.

The Nature of the Fetus

It is doubtful that you will find explicitly stated anywhere in any recent psychological study on abortion that the investigator believes that the fetus is not a human being. This belief is presupposed. I do not intend to present here the manifold evidence attesting to the fact that the unborn child is a human being; I merely wish to expose the fact that the psychological investigators do have a bias in this area. Although their presupposition is never actually stated, one nonetheless catches countless glimmers of it below the surface. A small example: why, when a woman who has undergone an abortion speaks of the loss of her baby, do the investigators put quotation marks around "baby," but themselves write of the protoplasmic mass or the fetus, unencumbered by these small but significant type markings? It is because they assume that the aborted fetus is not a human being and they wish to impose this belief subtly upon their readers. Such an assumption not only affects the interpretation of the data collected, but it affects the actual data. For example, a woman's response to the question, "How do you feel about the recent therapeutic removal of the protoplasmic mass from your uterus?" would be different from her response to the question, "How do you feel about the recent murder of your unborn child?" *Which question is objective depends upon which one is true to the facts.* If abortion is indeed the killing of human beings, then to phrase the question any differently than the second alternative would be dissembling. If the basic assumption, which influences the method of study, is wrong, the interpretations and conclusions will most certainly be suspect.

I will present a study by two psychiatrists that clearly illustrates how their assumption concerning the nature of the unborn child biases their investigation. The study is entitled "Abortions and Acute Identity Crises in Nurses" and deals with "acute psychological reactions" suffered by nurses in response to their abortion work. This study reports: "All suffered from strong emotional reactions to their abortion work . . . In varying degrees they all showed symptoms of anxiety and depression. They complained about being tired and being unhappy about their work; they cried too easily and got angry too quickly; they had difficulty sleeping and had bad dreams; during the day they found themselves preoccupied with disturbing thoughts about their abortion work; and they were overly sensitive when their friends teased them about working in a "slaughter house" . . . They were confused and uncertain about their role and function as nurses and no longer felt proud of their hospital and their work."[1] If abortion is indeed the killing of small human beings, then the nurses' reactions are not at all surprising. The anxiety and depression they exhibited are common symptoms of a guilty conscience. If abortion is murder, in which they have assisted, then they *should* have guilty consciences because they *are* guilty. Especially since many of the nurses had been pro-abortion before they actually took part in one, their reactions could have been used as an indicator that the moral issue in abortion needed reevaluation. However, the investigators had already concluded that the unborn child was not a human being, nor was its destruction immoral. Therefore, another explanation of the nurses' reactions had to be posited. The explanation was merely this: "The nurses' symptomatology fell in the category of a transient reactive disorder."[2]

The report continues to say that the nurses overidentified with and overreacted to the aborted fetus. Authors Char and McDermott record that "a most disturbing experience to the nurses was to hold a well-formed aborted fetus with movement and with its eyes 'still alive' . . . Some of the nurses overreacted when they allegedly saw formed fetal parts such as hair and bits of limbs being sucked out or scraped out. The nurses who overidentified with the fetus projected into the protoplasmic masses real, live, grown-up individuals."[3] *Protoplasmic masses? Alleged fetal parts?* What did they think the nurses saw? Parts of a grapefruit? It would be most disturbing if a human being were *not* disturbed at the sight of such atrocities. The nurses were the ones responding humanly to the reality of the situation. It was the investigators who, when confronted with facts that gave the lie to their presuppositions, resorted to denial, distortion, and deception. By couching their findings in professional psychological terminology, they attempted—successfully—to camouflage the real issues.

The authors conclude that the nurses' "symptoms came from an acute identity crisis that they suffered as a result of their abortion work. In the past they were supposed to save and bring forth life. Now they were supposed to terminate life. In the past as good nurses they cared for their patients and wanted to help them. Now they wanted to reject them. In the past they respected physicians and willingly carried out their orders. Now they were angry at and had doubts about physicians. All these factors severely threatened their traditional image of what a good nurse should be."[4] If one begins with the assumption that the unborn child is not a human being and that abortion is therefore not murder, then "identity crisis" becomes a plausible explanation. If abortion is murder, however, the explanation is simple and the nurses' reactions understandable. Indeed, if they did not react with guilt about their work, sorrow for their victim, and anger, doubt, resentment, and rejection

28

toward the murderers, the problem would be more complicated and less understandable.

The outcome for the nurses in this hospital was tragic. Char and McDermott state that they regained "objectivity about abortions . . . They saw again that what is aborted is a proto-plasmic mass and not a real, live . . . individual . . . Abortion is now considered a matter of routine."[5] The psychiatrists were effective. The nurses did not follow the wise saying: "Believe what your eyes see and not what your ears hear." They listened to the psychiatrists and were persuaded that what they saw they did not see and what they knew they did not know. The psychiatrists, backed by the authority of the science of the human psyche, explained to the nurses the cause of the quiver-ing of their souls—"identity crisis"—and the nurses allowed their consciences to be stilled and their senses dulled by the voice of the expert. It is not only the nurses in this hospital who have been silenced; an entire nation, duped by the propaganda of the professional elite, now considers abortion a matter of routine.

The Nature of Morality

Another presupposition that permeates the psychological studies on abortion concerns the nature of reality in the moral sphere. Psychological investigators assume that morality is not governed by absolute, immutable, universal, God-given laws. They assume instead that moral sanctions are relative, altera-ble, cultural, man-made. Professionals who survey the psycho-logical studies on abortion are searching for "consistency and consensus" among the investigators, to aid in the establish-ment of the new abortion ethic. But if the nature of reality is such that moral laws exist independently of human apprecia-tion or approval of them, then "consistency and consensus" are meaningless and man's legalization or moralization of the transgressions against these laws will avail nothing; they will remain unrepealed, unrevoked—and man, the creature who claimed to be the maker and measure of all morals, will himself be measured by them. He will be guilty, regardless of the so-phisticated sanctions he has created for himself.

This presupposition about the nature of morality surfaces in the recent studies on the psychological effects of abortion most often and most clearly in relation to the question of guilt. Traditional psychiatry has always viewed guilt as a product of unconscious, unresolved conflict in the individual resulting from the transgression of mythical taboos laid down by society. It assumes that there is no absolute standard of right and wrong, and thus no falling short of that standard, no ensuing true and moral guilt with all its psychological consequences and manifestations. If one views guilt according to the traditional psychiatric model, it is a constricting and damaging state for the individual and must therefore be alleviated (as was seen in the case of the hospital nurses). If, however, it is accurate that guilt can be true and moral, a consequence of a true and moral transgression; if it is true that both the guilt and the transgression are real, then psychiatry has gone astray in its understanding and resolution of this human dilemma. By helping a patient to "feel better" when, in fact, he is morally culpable, the psychiatrist has deceived his patient about the true nature of his condition. Psychological explanations provide a convenient escape and a comfortable illusion for the patient, for the counselor, and for society.

It is interesting to note in the recent abortion studies how the psychiatric investigators view the guilt feelings of the patient. They betray their basic beliefs by the conclusions they reach. Let us examine their interpretations of the various postabortion reactions:

1. If a woman, after receiving an abortion, does not feel guilty, it is concluded that she has responded favorably to the procedure. Most women in the recent abortion studies do not report that they feel guilty, but rather that they feel "better." The investigators conclude, therefore, that abortion is "therapeutic."[6] One can only arrive at that conclusion if one begins with the assumption that "not feeling guilty" is psychologically healthy. An investigator who believes that morality is absolute, and that a person can *be* guilty without *feeling* guilty, and that a woman who has consented to the murder of her own offspring *is* guilty and *ought* to feel guilty would arrive at exactly the opposite conclusion. For him, the absence of postabortion guilt feelings would be a clear indication that abortion (aside from being morally wrong) is extremely dangerous to a woman's psychological health, because it dulls her moral sensitivity and deadens her conscience. This is clearly illustrated by the experience of a counselee of C.F. Bajema, recorded in his book *Abor-*

30

tion and the Meaning of Personhood. It concerns a girl who had had a suction abortion and was invited by her doctor to view the "fetal remains" in a jar. "This particular girl reported that she 'felt nothing' when she viewed the torn-up aborted child. She claimed she felt no guilt whatsoever. In fact, what bothered her was precisely the *absence* of any guilt feeling. The numbness and hardness of her spirit, for which she had gradually conditioned herself, scared her and made her feel 'one' with the 'butchers at Buchenwald' who could view heaps of dead bodies in mass graves and not 'feel a thing.' "[7]

2. If a woman does feel somewhat guilty after an abortion, her doubts are referred to as "minor," her guilt "mild," her depression "transient," and her feelings of regret or loss "temporary." These "minor negative feelings" are nothing of psychological consequence. The investigators readily conclude that "abortion was genuinely therapeutic" and that "on the whole, the experience led to further emotional maturity and resolution of conflict."[8] One wonders what kind of maturity the psychiatrists are promoting by encouraging a woman to deal with such a great responsibility by abandoning it and to resolve her conflicts about motherhood and ambivalence about childbearing by destroying her child. But aside from that question, it is also interesting to note that in the present pro-abortion climate, a woman who feels guilty and admits it to herself and others is opposing the most highly esteemed experts of the entire nation. She is contradicting all those authorities who have declared her "not guilty." The sages of the Supreme Court have declared that abortion is just. The leaders of the women's liberation movement have proclaimed that this is the way to freedom. The clergy of the liberal church have pronounced their ecclesiastical blessing upon the act. The medical profession has raised a blood-stained hand in approval and those whose area of expertise is the human psyche have enlightened the woman to the therapeutic nature of this experience. Who would dare to defy such authorities? And yet, occasionally, a woman still feels uneasy—just a vague unrest within her voices itself in an unsure whisper. But who can hear a whisper of protest amidst the roar of approval? Who can hear the voice of conscience within when outside the applause grows deafening? One would think that any expression of guilt or doubt (however slight), when it opposes the established abortion ethic, would be of great psychological consequence to the investigators, but it

31

is no longer in their interest to explore this. The most important consideration they have ignored altogether: that guilt feelings, however mild and transitory, may relate to the real transgression of a true moral law that exists independently of our belief in it or adherence to it. The guilt feelings may not be severe or permanent. But the guilt itself is.

3. If a woman does experience an acute guilt reaction or severe psychiatric disturbance after an abortion, the psychological profession concludes that the problem lies with the woman and her previous mental state, not with the "therapeutic" procedure of abortion. These postabortion disturbances are said to be "related to existent psychopathology, rather than to the procedure."[9] What great strides the pro-abortion movement has taken! First we were assured that abortion was only for the mentally unstable; now we are informed that abortion is therapeutic for the mentally healthy! By controlling the definitions and implications of "psychological health," the psychological profession is able to influence the course of society and ultimately to attain the goals the profession desires—in this case, legalized abortion. When a woman reports a severe negative reaction to abortion, her subjective experience is now questioned and requires further validation by the investigator. For example, in one follow-up study of women who had undergone legal abortions, it was noted that "65 percent of the women stated that they were satisfied with their abortion and had no self-reproaches . . . 11 percent said they had a serious degree of self-reproach or regretted having had the operation." Of this latter group the investigator notes that "even though the women themselves reported a severe reaction, from a psychiatric point of view the reactions were considered mild."[10] The woman's subjective appraisal, when consistent with the psychiatric investigator's view, is accepted, whereas those subjective views which are inconsistent with his are reinterpreted.

It seems that however contradictory the evidence, the psychiatric investigator is always able to arrive at his own desired conclusions. By controlling the definitions and reinterpreting the evaluations, he is able to make pathological that which is normal, and normal that which is pathological. He is able to reconstruct the information to support his own presuppositions and society's changing cultural values and legal norms.

Daniel Callahan reviews the studies on the psychological reactions to abortion in his book *Abortion: Law, Choice, and*

Morality. He succinctly expresses the moral relativist's point of view in his recommendation: "It seems to me, therefore, that however vague and unsatisfactory the psychiatric knowledge of the effect of abortion, a sensitive psychiatrist might well conclude, concerning a given patient, that she will be able to undergo abortion with little or no serious guilt. Concerning another patient, he might conclude that her background and situation make a serious guilt reaction likely . . . he could well be correct in both instances."[11] If morals are absolute, both conclusions cannot be correct. One recommendation would be right, the other wrong, regardless of the patient's reaction. It is clearly evident from this statement that Callahan sees the guilt feelings as the problem and not the act that elicits such feelings. If the act of abortion transgresses an absolute moral law, making those who take part in it guilty, then the presence or absence of guilt feelings is irrelevant. The problem is whether they are guilty, not whether they feel guilty. The problem is whether they have transgressed a moral boundary, not whether they feel remorse for this transgression. If human beings have been endowed with a sensitivity to universal and absolute moral laws, if they possess an indicator (i.e., a conscience) that informs them when they have transgressed these laws, it would be foolishness to concentrate on the indicator rather than the indication. It would make as much sense for a mechanic to work on disconnecting the flashing red light on one's automobile dashboard rather than correcting the real problem that the warning light is signaling.

In general, the psychological studies on abortion reflect a basic belief about the nature of morality. The very criterion they use to validate their position on abortion (i.e., subjective experience) stems from an unvalidated belief about the nature of morality. That one person's subjective appraisal of well-being should be elevated to the status of the deciding criterion for life or death is a selfish hedonism. It is nothing less than moral perversity and total corruption. Human feelings are too complicated and deceptive to furnish a basis upon which to legislate morality. If they are used, the result is floundering in the quicksand of changing human perception, rather than standing on the firm ground of eternal God-given laws. The psychiatric investigators themselves admit that uncertainties and unreliable conclusions plague their experimental studies and yet, notwithstanding this uncertainty, they persist in using a subjective standard—and they persist in supporting abortion. Callahan states: "Abortion is a nasty problem, a source of social and legal discord, moral uncertainty, medical and psychiatric confusion, and personal anguish."[12] One wonders why in such uncertainty it is for death that psychologists and psychiatrists have chosen. One wonders why in such confusion the command has not been to stop, but to proceed; and why those at the head of the procession wish to proceed faster. As one professor of obstetrics and gynecology declared: "Our real problem is that, as soon as we mention abortion, people think we are talking about sin or murder. Perhaps one of the greatest contributions that somebody could make is a new term . . . If we could call this something more acceptable than abortion, we could get the public's attitudes changed a little faster."[13]* This professor is wrong in his assessment of the situation. The real problem is whether abortion *is* sin or murder, but it seems that those who are marching to the cheer of "progressive social change" do not hesitate in their chant or falter in their step to ask the simple question: Is it right? Man cannot determine the answer alone. Discord, uncertainty, confusion, and anguish are the inevitable result of man's moral quest if he has no reference point outside of himself. If man's own thoughts, emotions, and desires are the highest court of appeal in moral conflict, we can expect nothing less than a continuation of the degeneration and destruction that have marked the history of man, for his intentions have been continually evil.

The Nature of Man

The question of the nature of man, whether he is basically good or evil, is a subject shrouded in suspicious silence. One would think that the nature of man would be of utmost interest to those representing the psychiatric-psychological profession, but nowhere in their studies on abortion is there even the hint of the existence of such a question, much less a discussion of it or an answer to it. What is the consensus behind their silence?

*One psychologist in his study did employ an interesting new term. He referred to abortions as "life-rationing activities." Henry P. David, "Abortion in Psychological Perspective," *American Journal of Orthopsychiatry* 42:1 (1972), p. 64.

If the consensus is that man is evil, why have they so casually supported a movement designed to abolish the legal restraints upon the expression of wickedness? If the consensus is that man is good, then they hold this belief contrary to historical evidence, personal experience, and biblical authority. Are the ears of the experts deafened to the warnings that echo from man's past? Have their eyes been blinded to the evil that faces us from every side and confronts us from within? Have their hearts been hardened to the Word of God spoken through the prophets? "The hearts of the sons of men are full of evil, and insanity is in their hearts throughout their lives."[14] "Thus says the Lord: Cursed is the man who trusts in mankind . . . The heart is more deceitful than all else and is desperately wicked."[15] "There is no one who does good . . . they have all turned aside; together they have become corrupt; there is no one who does good, not even one."[16] "There is nothing reliable in what they say . . . with their tongues they keep deceiving."[17] "Their feet run to evil, and they hasten to shed innocent blood; their thoughts are thoughts of iniquity; devastation and destruction are in their paths and they do not know the way of peace. There is no justice in their way: they have made their paths crooked."[18] "There is no fear of God before their eyes."[19] Even if they claim that neither good nor evil is a native quality inherent in the human race as a whole, their actions and other beliefs indicate their basic endorsement of the humanistic tenet that man is basically good. Their very notion that it is man who creates moral laws for himself presupposes the belief that man is capable of such a creation. However, if man's nature is wholly corrupt, he is not only unable to create moral laws, but unwilling to obey those which he knows are already in existence. The idea that man is evolving morally assumes that man is "progressing," which suggests forward movement and betterment. It assumes that man is changing and that the change involves enrichment and enlightenment. If man is essentially evil, however, he is stagnant in his wickedness and any progress is merely a new expression of this wickedness.

The assertion of the wickedness of man is extremely pertinent to the psychological perspective on abortion. Within it lies the answer to the motivational questions that arise as one reviews the abortion literature. Why? Why? Again and again the question arises, threatening to engulf one in the anguish of no answer. Why has death, instead of life, been chosen? Why have the nation's judges, in the name of justice, perverted the honor of their office by giving sanction to the murderer and a death sentence to the innocent? Why have those whose profession it is to save life used their prestige and medical skills to destroy life? Why have the social and psychological investigators, in the name of "progressive social change" and "individual mental health," chosen the slaughter of unborn children as their social "solution" and their method of "therapy"? Why have mothers, in the name of the liberation of womanhood, demanded the death of their own children? Why? Why, in defiance of all scientific evidence and sanctity-of-life ethics, has abortion been pursued? From the darkness of this human madness comes an answer that sheds light, that defines the darkness—human wickedness. Knowing good, man will choose evil. Having the knowledge that the unborn child is a human being and that taking its life is murder and a transgression of the Law, man will commit abortion anyway and he will do it under the guise of goodness.

The Nature of Reality

It is interesting to note, in reviewing *The Right to Abortion: A Psychiatric View* by the Group for the Advancement of Psychiatry, that the authors dismiss the arguments of an anti-abortion Catholic simply because, in the final analysis, his arguments are based upon his religious beliefs. The GAP writers state in their report: "There remains the moral issue of abortion as murder. We submit that this is insoluble—a matter of religious philosophy and religious principle and not a matter of fact."[20] This statement grows out of a sophisticated philosophical belief system, a dualism in which the "religious" is relegated to a realm of the unverifiable and unfactual. But this philosophical assumption is itself unverifiable and unfactual. They charge that their opponent's position is religious and therefore subjective and biased—"not a matter of fact." A religious belief is not necessarily unfactual; this depends upon whether or not it is true! They claim for themselves an objective and neutral position, but, according to their own definition, they are not objective or neutral, for they themselves operate within a religious system—that of materialistic, atheistic humanism. This is the philosophical foundation upon which all the investigations and recommendations of the GAP writers are built. Their psychological "contribution" to abortion is the product of a philosophical stance that rests precariously upon very little evidence. They deny the supernatural and spiritual dimension of reality. They deny the existence of a transcendent God and His revelation. They elevate man to a position of unlimited authority and autonomy—yet depreciate him to accommodate their self-construed, self-imposed definition of humanness. Ironically, abortion is the legitimate off-spring of humanism. "Thus says the Lord: Cursed is the man who trusts in mankind."[21] Abortion is surely just one manifestation of the curse we have incurred by forsaking God.

How, specifically, does the religion of materialistic-atheistic humanism influence psychiatry's position on abortion? One could choose many examples, but perhaps a discussion of the concept of freedom would prove most profitable. The GAP writers believe that a woman has "the right to abortion." The reason they are against restrictive abortion laws is that such laws deprive women of their liberty, but their notion of liberty is derived from their religious system. It is a notion of liberty in which man himself determines the boundaries of his free-dom. He has declared himself to be limitless; he has declared himself to be "free" to go beyond any boundary. His only re-straints are his capabilities, but as he progresses these too vanish in the blazing glory of his advance. Man is viewed as infinite in his capabilities and, ironically, finite in his worth. Hence the incredible contradiction in the pro-abortionist's ar-gument: man is so great that he can create his own standards to determine who shall live and who shall die—but man is so small that he can be casually discarded into the hospital incin-erator. Opposed to this view is the Christian position. Man is finite, but of infinite worth. Every human life (no matter how undeveloped, deformed, or detestable) is of immeasurable value. Man's worth is infinite—but he himself is finite. He is limited physically and spiritually. He is limited by his body, by the nature of his being, and by the moral laws of God. Neither men nor women have the right to transgress these boundaries. People may throw off their innermost restraints or forsake the law of God, but bondage is the result. In the beginning (Genesis 3) the enticement to sin was to add to one's being by crossing a barrier that appeared to be a limitation to humanness. But the result of the deception and the transgression was dehumanization and death. Bondage lay beyond the barrier. Freedom lay within the confines of God's law. Pro-abortionists employ a similar deception: "You need not be held back by your physical condition or your psychological conditioning . . . Go beyond . . ." And the result is the same. There is loss, not gain. This loss has been profoundly expressed by a girl who had two abortions. "She felt that the second abortion had literally scraped away the last vestiges of her own humanness and had left her with a totally empty self—not just an empty womb but an empty being."[22] Others also are aware of the loss. One anti-abortion group now calls itself "Women Exploited." Its members are women who have themselves undergone abortions and have perceived the deception. They were not liberated, but exploited.

The psychiatric-psychological profession continually speaks of women as having been "inhibited" by social and legal norms. But the question concerning abortion is: Are these merely cultural values that are inhibiting us? Is it merely social conditioning that is restricting us? Or is it something intrinsic to the human being that makes us hesitate? Are not the established experts attempting to reconstitute human nature? Are we not being bound by the new ethic that one can no longer allow oneself to be bound—even by our own consciences or the very nature of our being? It seems that we have become the slaves and the victims of the manipulations of those in power who are endeavoring to recondition people's thoughts and feelings to conform to that philosophy and course of action which they themselves have determined to be expedient. For example, in most of the present abortion studies "the major conclusion drawn is that in both a physical and psychological sense it is less traumatic to have an abortion than to bring the pregnancy to term."[23] The psychiatric-psychological profession, with its unchallenged control over the definition of "traumatic," has determined that it is no longer natural and normal for a woman to give birth. The experts have determined that the human birth process is unnatural, "traumatic," and potentially pathological. With one word they have robbed woman of her privileged position and purpose in human history. One word wielded with unlimited authority enables them to divert the God-given destiny of mankind from "Be fruitful and multiply and fill the earth" to a course of barrenness, destructiveness, and emptiness. Women beware! Beware of the liberators and the freedom they offer.

The Christian views abortion as an expression of human wickedness and an act of rebellion against God. Not only does it transgress God's law ("Thou shalt not murder"); abortion is an act designed to assault God by destroying the pinnacle of His creation, the creature made in His image—man. Any attack against human life is an attack against the One who is the Author of Life. The Christian views the present abortion craze not as an isolated event in the horror of human history, but as another expression of man's continuing rebellion against the Lord. This rebellion not only spans the entire age of human existence, but it encompasses realms beyond man's existence. In combating abortion one is engaging in a battle of cosmic proportions against an evil of incomprehensible dimensions. We are not merely struggling against the wickedness of the human heart, but "against the rulers, against the powers, against the forces of the darkness of this world, against the spiritual forces of wickedness in the heavenly places."[24]

For our sin we face the righteous wrath and the judgment of God. Man's rebellion against the Lord brings temporal and eternal consequences. In this life the results of sin are further depravity and death. Abortion is an expression of the depravity we have reaped for our sin of forsaking God. "For even though they knew God, they did not honor Him as God, or give thanks; but they became futile in their speculations, and their foolish heart was darkened. Professing to be wise, they became fools . . . Therefore God gave them over in the lusts of their hearts to impurity, that their bodies might be dishonored among them. For they exchanged the truth of God for a lie, and worshiped and served the creature rather than the Creator, who is blessed forever. Amen. For this reason God gave them over to degrading passions . . . and just as they did not see fit to acknowledge God any longer, God gave them over to a depraved mind, to do those things which are not proper . . ."[25] In this life the consequences of sin are further depravity and temporal death. In the life to come, the penalty for sin is eternal death and damnation. Man is enslaved, not by God's commands, but by his servitude to sin. Man is in bondage to sin and death; but, praise be to God, He has sent the Savior into the world, Jesus Christ, and "if the Son shall set you free, you shall be free indeed."[26]

What is the Christian solution to the problem of abortion? Repentance. The solution is to turn from the sin of committing murder by abortion and to turn from the false religion that approves abortion. The solution is to turn to the Lord and to keep His commandments.[27]

Notes

1. Walter F. Char, M.D. and John F. McDermott, Jr., M.D., "Abortions and Acute Identity Crises in Nurses," *American Journal of Psychiatry* 128:8 (1972), p. 67.

2. *Ibid.*

3. *Ibid.*

4. *Ibid.,* p. 70.

5. *Ibid.*

6. *Legalized Abortion and the Public Health Report* (Washington, D.C.: National Academy of Sciences, 1975), p. 92.

7. Clifford E. Bajema, *Abortion and the Meaning of Personhood* (Grand Rapids, Mich.: Baker Book House, 1974), p. 72.

8. *Legalized Abortion,* pp. 92, 93.

9. *Ibid.,* p. 93.

10. David Callahan, *Abortion: Law, Choice, and Morality* (London: Collier-Macmillan, 1970), p. 67.

11. *Ibid.,* p. 75.

12. *Ibid.,* p. 1.

13. Clyde Randall, *Abortion in a Changing World* (New York: Columbia University Press, 1970), 2:88.

14. Ecclesiastes 9:3.

15. Jeremiah 17:9.

16. Psalm 14:1, 3.

17. Psalm 5:9.

18. Isaiah 59:7, 8.

19. Psalm 36:1.

20. Group for the Advancement of Psychiatry, *The Right to Abortion: A Psychiatric View* (New York: Scribner's, 1970), p. 48.

21. Jeremiah 17:5.

22. Bajema, *Abortion and Meaning of Personhood,* p. 70.

23. William C. Brennan, "Abortion and the Techniques of Neutralization," *Journal of Health and Social Behavior,* 15 (1974), p. 361.

24. Ephesians 6:12.

25. Romans 1:18–32.

26. John 8:32.

27. Ecclesiastes 12:13.

3 Abortion from a Biblical Perspective

John M. Frame

Each day it becomes more and more urgent for the
Church to speak a word from God concerning the current drive
for liberalized abortion laws. If abortion is sin in any sense,
then we should be most concerned about the breadth and depth
of the desire for it in our culture. And if abortion is murder,
even in some cases, then the current pace of abortion liberalization could lead to a slaughter of defenseless human beings
worse than the atrocities of Hitler, Stalin, or Herod the Great.

Yet Christians have been reluctant to address this issue
boldly and forthrightly. Apart from that carnal timidity which
inhibits Christian witnessing on *all* issues, this reluctance may
be ascribed largely to two difficulties: (1) the difficulty of demonstrating from Scripture that the unborn child is, from conception, a human person whose right to life is protected by the
Sixth Commandment, and (2) the difficulty of reconciling the
rights of the unborn (however they may be construed) with
other concerns for which we find scriptural basis. Thus Christians have been tempted to back away from the abortion controversy, perhaps even to rest in the false consolation that our
present ignorance concerning the matter will excuse us of
blame for any evil resulting from our inaction. But God does
not excuse slothful and wilful ignorance, nor does He excuse us
of complicity in evil resulting from such ignorance. He calls us
in this as in all matters to search out the whole counsel of God,
to resolve our difficulties as much as Scripture allows, and to
proclaim the truth with confidence. I pray that God will use
this essay to help Christians resolve their problems in this area
and hence to purify and embolden their testimony.

In this paper, "abortion" will be used to refer to any intentional killing of a human embryo or fetus. For the sake of

simplicity, and to put the ethical issue at stake into sharper focus, this definition assigns to the term a broad meaning (instead of the narrower usage wherein abortion is distinguished from miscarriage and premature labor as an *early* termination of pregnancy). Further, the term will not be used to denote spontaneous abortion unless the adjective "spontaneous" accompanies it.

The greatest of the commandments is the law of love (Matthew 22:36–40 and parallels; John 13:34–35; Romans 13:8–10; Galatians 5:14). Our first obligation, therefore, in any ethical decision, is to manifest genuine love for God and for other people. In this context we must ask: Can a decision in favor of abortion (in general or in a particular situation) ever be an act of love? The question is a searching one; it forces us not only to dig deeply into Scripture but also to analyze the profoundest motives of our own hearts. Sometimes, however, decisions in favor of abortion are all too clear in their motivation. Sometimes the spirit of selfishness, of greed, of destruction, of hate is plain enough to be seen by all, except perhaps the one in whom that spirit dwells. When a woman decides in favor of abortion merely for convenience, or when a woman has an abortion simply to show that she can "do anything she wishes with her own body"—surely she is far from the spirit of the Lord Jesus Christ who humbled himself and even laid down his life for his friends. Here the motive is obvious to anyone with a basic understanding of Scripture. To such as these we need say no more before demanding repentance.

Yet sometimes the motives are not so obvious. Often, motives are mixed and the dominant motive is hard to find. Such difficulties should direct us back to the law of God for more clarification; for it is the Law that shows us what love does and what love does not do. Here of course we must beware of using exegesis as a means of rationalization: it is always tempting to read the Law in a Pharisaic way—using it to justify our wicked hearts by pointing to the formal correctness of our actions. Yet to the Christian the Law is indispensable; it is his final authority, the very Word of God Himself. Without the Law we would have no knowledge of love whatever, for love is itself a command and is defined in the context of all God's commands.

What, then, is the unborn child, according to Scripture? He is, first of all, a creature of God. Does that point seem too obvious to mention? Yet this affirmation alone is a decisive

44

rebuke to the spirit of human autonomy. The unborn child belongs (in the most ultimate sense) not to his parents, or to human society in general, or to government, but to God. No created thing is man's simply to use as he pleases, disregarding God's will. Man has dominion over the earth, to be sure; but this dominion was intended to be a covenant stewardship under God, not a usurpation of God's authority. Our present environmental crisis shows vividly how sin corrupts man's rightful dominion into a lustful and destructive tyranny. To say that the unborn child is ours to treat as we please is to give less consideration to the child than God demands we give to rivers and rocks.

But the unborn child is more than a river or a rock, more than other creatures of God: he is a *living* creature, one possessing a divinely granted sovereignty over the inanimate creation (Genesis 1). Along with other living creatures, he stands under the protection of God's covenant with Noah (Genesis 9:9–10). The blood of even subhuman living creatures had a special preciousness in the Old Testament period: since the blood of an animal represented its divinely created *life*, such blood was not to be consumed by man (Leviticus 17:14), and the shedding of it was the God-appointed means of prefiguring the atoning work of Christ (Leviticus 17:11). In these ordinances God required of His people a careful regard for the lives of all of His creatures, even those whose lives were to be sacrificed to meet the needs of man. Man's dominion over *living* creatures is even more explicitly limited in Scripture than is his dominion over the inanimate world.

But the unborn child is more even than a merely "living" creature: he is *human* life, and therefore a bearer of the image of God. Some indeed may wish to argue that he is not an *independent* human life because he functions as a part of his mother's body—this argument we shall discuss later. But even if the child is not an independent human life, there can be no doubt that he is *human*—just as human, at least, as his mother's arms or legs. It must not be supposed that at some point between conception and birth the child develops uniquely human characteristics in the place of uniquely subhuman ones. From the point of conception, he has a full complement of human chromosomes and is in that respect different from every subhuman embryo or fetus. From the very beginning, he is a human child, and his humanity is verifiable in every cell of his body.

Now even if the unborn child were merely a part of his mother's body, he would still be a bearer of the image of God. The image of God pertains to all aspects of man's being, the physical included. According to Scripture it is man himself, not merely some aspect of man, that is made in the image of God. This fact places the unborn child under a specific scriptural protection, for the biblical prohibition of murder is based upon the presence of the image of God in man (Genesis 9:6). And according to the Westminster Shorter Catechism, the prohibition of murder forbids not only "the taking away of our own life or the life of our neighbor unjustly," but also "whatsoever tendeth thereunto" (Q. 69), which according to the Larger Catechism includes "striking" and "wounding" (Q. 136). Since man is made in the image of God, therefore, he has no unlimited sovereignty over his own body (cf. I Corinthians 6:15–7:4). He may not harm or wound it without just cause. To say, then, that the unborn child is part of his mother's body is not to offer an excuse for destroying him, but rather to establish a presumption in favor of preserving him.

But still more must be said. The unborn child is not merely human life, significant though that fact may be. He is a product of the human reproductive system. Throughout Scripture, man's sexual life is a matter of particular divine concern. The Bible is nowhere more emphatic in its condemnation of pretended human autonomy than in its teaching concerning sex. The sacredness of the sexual relation is indicated often in Scripture: immediately after the statement that man was created in God's image, we learn of his sexual differentiation (Genesis 1:27). The first effect of sin noted in the account of the Fall is sexual shame (Genesis 3:7, 10). The Mosaic law not only demanded marital fidelity, but also placed ceremonial sanctions upon various sexual functions: male emissions and female menstruation, as well as the event of childbirth itself, were causes for ceremonial uncleanness (Leviticus 12, 15, 18:6–23, 20:10–21). The New Testament, too, demands that sexual activity be kept within certain bounds. Its condemnation of "sins against the body" and its teaching that neither husband nor wife has "power over his own body" both occur in a context dealing specifically with sexual conduct (I Corinthians 6:15–7:7). The importance of this sexual purity is underscored by the fact that the marriage relation mirrors the relation between Christ and the Church. If God is so jealous to maintain His lordship in this

46

area of human life, is it conceivable that the product of sexual intercourse—the unborn child—should be wholly consigned to the whims of his parents?

Our rhetorical question must indeed be answered in the negative: for God is concerned not only with human sexual activity as such, but also with the *result* of that activity in the conception of children. Man's reproductive function plays a crucial role both in man's cultural task (Genesis 1:28, the command to be fruitful and multiply) and in the promise of redemption (which is from the outset of redemptive history the promise of *seed,* Genesis 3:15). The faith of Eve is demonstrated particularly in connection with her childbearing (Genesis 4:1,25). The Abrahamic (Genesis 15:1–5) and the Davidic (II Samuel 7:12–16) covenants contain explicit promises of seed, and the other Old Testament covenants presuppose such promises. The Old Testament abounds in genealogies, demonstrating the historical development of the "seed of the promise" through the birth of children, a development that reaches its culmination in the birth of Christ (Matthew 1:1–17, Luke 3:23–38). It is in this context that we should understand the biblical regulation of sexual activity and also the profound conviction of the biblical saints that conception was a precious gift of God while barrenness was a curse (Genesis 4:1, 25; 21:1–2; 25:21; 29:31–35; 30:-17–24; 33:5; Deuteronomy 7:13; 28:4; Judges 13:2–7; I Samuel 1:1–20; Ruth 4:13; Psalms 113:9; 127:3–5; 128:1–6; Isaiah 54:1; Luke 1:24; in more profound sense, cf. Matthew 1:20, Luke 1:31). Although the physical genealogy of the redemptive line ends in Christ, the New Testament continues to regard the children of believers as a spiritual as well as a temporal blessing. God still carries out His redemptive purposes through the drawing of households to Himself (Acts 11:14, 16:15, 16:31–34, 18:8), the children of which are "holy" (I Corinthians 7:14). God has, therefore, a definite, personal, even redemptive concern with the event of conception, for by conception He has determined to bless His people and to build up His kingdom on earth. In this context the question of abortion becomes: In what cases, if ever, is it legitimate for us to destroy what God has created to bless His people and to build up His church? Also: In what cases, if ever, is the attitude of one planning abortion compatible with the biblical "joy in conception"? These questions are not entirely rhetorical; we have not yet answered them as fully as they can be answered. Yet, asked in the right spirit, they provide an important context for our thinking on this issue.

But God is not only active in the event of conception itself. He is directly involved in all aspects of the child's development between conception and birth. In Psalm 139:13–16, David reflects on the amazing knowledge and wisdom by which God formed his body in the womb of his mother. (Note that verse 16 contains the only occurrence in Scripture of the Hebrew term *golem,* embryo or fetus.) In Jeremiah 1:5, the prophet is said to have been "formed in the belly" of his mother by God. (Cf. in this connection Job 31:15, Psalm 119:73, Ecclesiastes 11:5.) The gestation period is ruled throughout by God's providence and care. To those considering abortion, therefore, we must ask: When, if at all, does man have the right to interrupt this marvelous exhibition of God's wisdom and concern?

Still further, prenatal death is regarded in Scripture as a particularly terrible form of that *curse* which rests upon man because of sin. God threatens Israel with precisely this curse because of their faithlessness (Hosea 9:14) and conversely promises to bless His people not only with conceptions, but with live births as a consequence of obedience (Exodus 23:26). Upon the wicked God's judgment is that they shall be "as an untimely birth" (Psalm 58:8). One of the worst things that can be said of a man in Scripture is that he is no better than an untimely birth (Job 3:10–16, 10:18–19; Ecclesiastes 6:3; cf. Matthew 26:24; Mark 14:21; Jeremiah 20:14–18). In I Corinthians 15:8, Paul uses the term *ektroma,* untimely birth (perhaps as it had been used by his critics—it occurs only here in Scripture), to acknowledge dramatically the "unnaturalness," the "unexpectedness," the "inappropriateness" of his apostolic calling. Paul had not followed Jesus through His earthly ministry, nor had he witnessed the original Resurrection appearances, or heard Jesus' teaching during the "forty days," or witnessed the Ascension. Rather, after these great events Paul had set himself against Christ, persecuting the Church. Thus God appeared to him, not as to one prepared by his faithful participation in this redemptive history to preach the gospel, but as to one spiritually dead, untimely born, "aborted." Here, as throughout Scripture, death before birth is an object of horror, a curse, a consequence of sin. In this context the abortion question becomes: When, if at all, does man have the right, not only to interrupt God's prenatal care for the unborn, but to interrupt this process in order to impose upon the child that

48

fate which is almost a paradigmatic emblem of divine curse?

Yet more, Scripture assumes a significant personal continuity between prenatal and postnatal human life. In Psalm 139: 13, David sees *himself* as existing in his mother's womb: "For thou didst form *my* inward parts: Thou didst cover *me* in my mother's womb." In Jeremiah 1:5, similar language is used, this time with God himself as the speaker: "Before I formed *thee* in the belly I knew *thee,* and before *thou* camest out of the womb I sanctified *thee . . .*" (emphasis mine here and in all scriptural citations). It was Jeremiah himself in the womb that God was forming; and God was forming him with a view toward the carrying out of his adult responsibilities. In the New Testament we learn that John the Baptist, while still in his mother's womb (in the sixth month of her pregnancy or later—cf. Luke 1:24, 26) responded to the salutation of Mary in a way befitting the character of his later ministry (Luke 1:41, 44). This event should not, of course, be construed as the natural, usual course of events; clearly the incident is an extraordinary sign of Jesus' lordship. Yet it presupposes the sort of continuity between prenatal and postnatal life that we have noted above: John in the womb is called *brephos,* a babe, and is said to have leapt "for joy." Such is indeed the general pattern of scriptural usage; for those in the womb are commonly referred to in Scripture by the same language used of persons already born (cf. Genesis 25:22, 38:27ff.; Job 1:21, 3:3, 11ff., 10:18–19, 31:15; Isaiah 44:2, 24, 49:5; Jeremiah 20:14–18; Hosea 12:3. See also references below). At the very least, this continuity indicates that God is not only forming and caring for the unborn child; He is forming him as a specific individual, to fit him specifically for his postnatal calling. This continuity is a warning against distinguishing with careless sharpness between fetal and infant life. And the abortion question now becomes: When, if at all, has man the right to destroy an unborn child, thereby cutting off the life of an individual who is being divinely prepared to play a particular role in God's world?

And that personal continuity extends back in time to the point of conception. Psalm 51:5 clearly and strikingly presses this continuity back to the point of conception. In this passage David is reflecting on the sin in his heart that had recently taken the form of adultery and murder. He recognizes that the sin of his heart is not itself a recent phenomenon, but goes back to the point of his conception in the womb of his mother: "and in sin did my mother conceive me." The personal continuity between David's fetal life and his adult life goes back as far as conception, and extends even to his ethical relation to God!

Yet in order to present the matter as clearly as possible, it must also be said that there is also a personal continuity which extends from adult life backwards in time even before conception and into eternity. God knew Jeremiah, not only after his conception, but even before it: *"Before* I formed thee in the belly I knew *thee"* (Jeremiah 1:5). The incarnate Son of God was given his name by the angel before his actual conception, that is, before his actual incarnation (Luke 2:21). Levi is said to have paid tithes to Melchizedek while still "in the loins of" his great-grandfather Abraham (Hebrews 7:9–10). All of these assertions are true because of the sovereignty of God who works all things after the counsel of his own will (Ephesians 1:11). Before anyone is actually conceived in the womb, God has planned the course of his life and his eternal destiny. Of God's elect it can be said that "he chose *us* in (Christ) *before the foundation of the world"* (Ephesians 1:4). Even *before* their conception, therefore, Scripture speaks of people in the language used of persons already born. All of us, even before we "exist," have a kind of "personal existence" as ideas in the mind of God. We shall make a negative application of this principle at a later point. At this point, however, let us note a positive implication: human life in the womb is a certain stage in the realization of an eternal plan. Even before conception, God sees, as it were, the "finished product"—the complete man with all his gifts and characteristics, in his belief or unbelief, fitted for blessing or destruction. Conception itself, as well as the gestation process, is in every aspect oriented to the fulfillment of that plan. If indeed the child should die before birth, then that is itself a result of God's plan. But such death is closely analogous to infant death (and for that matter to all human death), for it is the death of one whom God up to that point had cared for, preserved, and blessed; and it is the death of one who, had he not died, would have grown further toward mature humanity, toward the accomplishment of mature human goals. In this light the abortion question becomes: What human being will dare to take the responsibility for such death upon himself?

There is *nothing* in Scripture that even remotely suggests that the unborn child is anything less than a human person from the moment of conception. The only passage that has been alleged to make such a suggestion is Exodus 21:22–25, which I will now discuss in some detail. Those who use this passage to support the thesis that the unborn child is something less than a human person interpret it as follows. They see the 22nd verse as describing the destruction of an unborn child and find it significant that such destruction is punished only by a fine while harm done to the mother (23–25) merits more severe penalties, including the death penalty in the event of her death. On this account the passage may be paraphrased: "And if men fight together and hurt a pregnant woman so that her child dies, yet she herself is not harmed, he shall be surely fined, according as the woman's husband shall lay upon him; and he shall pay as the judges determine. But if the woman herself is harmed, then thou shalt give life for life, eye for eye, tooth for tooth, hand for hand, foot for foot, burning for burning, wound for wound, stripe for stripe." On this view the child is given a "lesser value" than the mother and is therefore regarded as something less than a human person.

This use of Exodus 21:22–25 raises questions in the following areas: (1) the normativity of this piece of Old Testament civil legislation for the New Testament church, (2) the adequacy of the interpretation of the passage used in this argument, (3) the legitimacy of the use of the passage so interpreted to prove the thesis that the unborn child is something less than a human person, and (4) the legitimacy of the use of this thesis to justify in at least some cases the practice of abortion. We shall take up these four questions in reverse order.

Even if the passage does prove the thesis in question, this fact does not prove that abortion is ever justified. Even if the unborn child is something less than a human person, this status does not justify his destruction under all, or some, or even *any* circumstances. We have already presented considerations directed against the destruction of the unborn that do not presuppose his status as a human being in the fullest sense. To justify abortion, even if we regard the unborn child as less than a person, those considerations must be refuted, or at least they must be shown to be overriden by other principles in the case in question.

Also relevant to question (4) is the teaching of the passage under consideration (granting the adequacy of the proposed interpretation). For it must not be forgotten that on any interpretation, the passage regards the destruction of the unborn as an offense, a wrong, a sin. In the absence of any other scriptural teaching that would establish exceptions to or modifications of the condemnation issued in this passage, it is perverse indeed to attempt to justify abortion by reference to a passage that condemns precisely the sort of destruction performed by the abortionist. The importance of the fact that, on the proposed interpretation, a lighter penalty is attached to the destruction of the unborn than to harm done the mother must not be overestimated. The Christian cannot justify committing sin on the ground that his sin is less heinous than other kinds of sin.

Again, granting the normativity, the interpretation, and the thesis asserted in the argument, this passage clearly deals with a case of _accidental_ killing. If even such accidental killing of an unborn child is punished by a fine, we must surely assume that the _intentional_ killing of an unborn child is at least as serious as (in all probability more serious than) the offense in view in verse 22. This fact makes it all the more perverse to defend abortion (on our definition, the intentional destruction of the unborn) on the basis of this passage. How can we defend the intentional destruction of the unborn on the basis of a passage which condemns even its accidental destruction?

One might object at this point that there are other scriptural considerations that would require exceptions to the general rule given in this passage. In such an event, such consideration might be combined with the "thesis" (above, question 3) obtained from this passage to produce a justification for a particular abortion. We are not concerned to deny such a possibility now, only to make clear that this passage taken _in itself_ does nothing to justify any practice of abortion, even if the other questions regarding this argument can be answered satisfactorily.

But we must now move on to question (3). Does the passage prove the thesis that the unborn child is less than a human person, granted the proposed interpretation? The argument is that since there is a lesser penalty for destruction of the child than for harm done to the mother, the child must have been regarded as "less than a human person." But this inference is not a sound one. The rationale for the various penalties assessed in the Mosaic law is an interesting and complicated subject, concerning which there is much room for debate. That the disparity in punishment must be due to a disparity between personhood and nonpersonhood is an interesting thesis, but cannot be simply assumed without argument. And there are, in our view, no arguments that render necessary such a conclusion.

The lack of a death penalty for destruction of the unborn in verse 22 does nothing to support the thesis in question. The law of Moses did not as a rule impose a mandatory death penalty in cases of accidental killing (cf. Exodus 21:13–14, 20–21). If indeed the law does impose such a penalty for the destruction of the mother's life (verse 23, "life for life"), then we have in this passage not a devaluation of the life of the child, but an extraordinary valuation upon the life of the mother, doubtless to give her (and her unborn child!) special protection throughout her pregnancy.

That there is no mention in verse 22 of an "avenger of blood" and of "cities of refuge" (after the pattern of other passages dealing with accidental killing, Numbers 35:10–34; Deuteronomy 19:1–13; cf. Exodus 21:13–14) does not demonstrate the thesis in question. No one doubts that the accidental killing of an unborn child is a unique case, one that might very well have failed to arouse the blood vengeance presupposed in the "cities of refuge" passages. The question, however, is whether this uniqueness is due to the child's lack of personhood. And that question cannot be answered by the presence or absence of the vengeance formulae.

But does not the very lightness of the penalty serve to establish the thesis in question? I think not. The immediately preceding passage (Exodus 21:20–21), in fact, presents a situation where a master who kills his slave unintentionally (the lack of intent being proved by the interval between the blow and the death) escapes with no penalty at all. To argue from this passage that slaves are regarded by God as less than human persons would be precarious indeed! To argue from Exodus 21:22–25 that the unborn child is not a person is even less plausible. Doubtless the unborn child, like the slave, had a lesser status in Israelite society than other persons. It cannot be demonstrated, however, that this lesser status was a status of nonpersonhood. And that is the point at issue.

If in spite of the above considerations we choose to regard the passage as establishing the thesis in question, then some serious consequences must be faced. The passage makes no distinction between embryo and fetus, none between viable and nonviable fetuses. All unborn children are reckoned equally in its teaching. If this passage is taken to prove that the unborn child is less than a person, then this conclusion must be taken to hold for *all* unborn children, even those who have been in the womb a full nine months! Depending on the extent to which this principle is understood as a guide to the practice of abortion, this view could result in the killing of a child ten minutes before its expected birth on the ground that it is not "really a person." If we accept the thesis under discussion, we may be forced to smother our natural repugnance to such a practice. It is of course true that Scripture requires us to adopt viewpoints that are repugnant to our sensibilities, when those sensibilities are not themselves sanctified. But we should not adopt a position without facing squarely the consequences; and if they cannot be reconciled with other aspects of our sensibilities, we should return to Scripture until the problem is resolved.

We now turn to question (2): Does the argument in question rest upon an adequate interpretation of Exodus 21:22–25? I would answer in the negative. In the first place, the term *yeled* in verse 22 never refers elsewhere to a child lacking recognizable human form, or to one incapable of existing outside the womb. The possibility of such a usage here, as the interpretation in question requires, is still further reduced by the fact that if the writer had wanted to speak of an undeveloped embryo or fetus, there may have been other terminology available to him. There was the term *golem* (Psalm 139:16) which means "embryo, fetus." But in cases of the death of an unborn child, Scripture regularly designates him, not by *yeled*, not even by *golem*, but by *nefel* (Job 3:16; Psalm 58:8; Ecclesiastes 6:3), "one untimely born." The use of *yeled* in verse 22, therefore, indicates that the child in view is not the product of a miscarriage, as the interpretation in question supposes; at least this is the most natural interpretation in the absence of decisive considerations to the contrary. (The reason for the plural form is difficult to assess on any interpretation. If, as some have suggested, it refers to the woman's capacity for bearing, then the passage becomes quite irrelevant to the matter of abortion. If, as is more likely, it is a plural of indefiniteness, allowing for the possibility of more than one child in the mother's body, then the plurality of the term would fit as easily into our interpretation as into the interpretation under criticism.)

Further, the verb *yatza'* in verse 22 ("go out," translated "depart" in KJV) does not in itself suggest the death of the child and is ordinarily used to describe normal births (Genesis 25:26, 38:28–30; Job 3:11, 10:18; Jeremiah 1:5, 20:18). With the possible exception of Numbers 12:12, which almost certainly refers to a stillbirth, it never refers to a miscarriage. The Old Testament term normally used for miscarriage and spontaneous abortion, both in humans and in animals, is not *yatza'* but *shakol* (Exodus 23:26; Hosea 9:14; Genesis 31:38; Job 2:10; cf. II Kings 2:19, 21; Malachi 3:11). The most natural interpretation of the phrase *wᵉyatzᵉ'u yᵉladheyha,* therefore, will find in it not an induced miscarriage, not the death of an unborn child, but an induced premature birth, wherein the child is born alive, but ahead of the anticipated time.

We should also note that the term *ason* ("harm"), found in both verse 22 and verse 23 is indefinite in its reference. The expression *lah* ("to her"), which would restrict the harm to the woman as opposed to the child, is missing. Thus the most natural interpretation would regard the "harm" as pertaining either to the woman or to the child. Verse 22 therefore describes a situation where neither mother nor child is "harmed"—i.e., where the mother is uninjured and the child is born alive. Verse 23 describes a situation where some harm *is* done—either to mother or child or both. This point confirms the interpretation I am advocating. An induced miscarriage could hardly be described as a situation where there is "no harm." Verse 22, therefore, describes, not an induced miscarriage, but an induced premature birth. A further implication of this reading of *ason:* when punishments are assessed in verses 23–25, the unborn child is protected, as is his mother, by the law of retaliation. The passage does not, of course, demonstrate that the child is given the same protection as his mother under this law; but it is clear that he is protected, that harm done to him is punished by some sort of retaliation, and thus that even his accidental destruction is wrong in the sight of God. If indeed other scriptural considerations require exceptions to this principle, then perhaps abortion might in some cases be justifiable; but this passage taken in itself offers no encouragement to any proposed abortion. On the contrary, the bearing of the passage upon the question is quite otherwise.

The reason for the fine in verse 22 is difficult to assess, but no more difficult on my interpretation than on any other. It is true that verse 22 does ordain a fine (*'anash*) rather than vengeance (*naqam*, as in the preceding passage, verse 20). Fines are not often assessed in the Mosaic law. The only other occurrence of *'anash* in the Pentateuch is in Deuteronomy 22:19, where a fine is assessed upon one who had "brought up an evil name upon a virgin of Israel." Could it be that premature birth was somehow considered shameful and that the fine in Exodus 21:22, in analogy with Deuteronomy 22:19, is a kind of damages for the harm done to the woman's reputation? Equally likely, the fine could be compensation for the trouble, expense, and danger involved in premature delivery. But to understand the precise reason for it, we would doubtless need more thorough understanding of Israelite culture than we now have. On the interpretation I am opposing, the fine would be compensation for the loss of an unborn child—a rather lenient penalty, it would seem, in view of the importance given to heirs and descendants in that culture, and in any case a penalty with no clear analogies elsewhere in Scripture. I am not dogmatic on this matter, but I think that the evidence available tends to confirm, rather than to undermine, the interpretation that I have established.

To summarize the proper interpretation of this passage, I would regard the following as an adequate paraphrase: "And if men fight together and hurt a pregnant woman so that her child is born prematurely, yet neither mother or child is harmed, he shall be surely fined, according as the woman's husband shall lay upon him; and he shall pay as the judges determine. But if either mother or child is harmed, then thou shalt give life for life, eye for eye, tooth for tooth, hand for hand, foot for foot, burning for burning, wound for wound, stripe for stripe."

One of our four questions remains, namely the question of the normativity of this passage for our present situation. Exodus 21:22–25 is part of the civil legislation given to Israel. Principles embedded in this legislation are not necessarily normative for New Testament believers. Consider Exodus 21:20–21, the immediately preceding passage. There we read that a slave can be killed by his master without penalty if the slave remains alive a day or two after the blow. This practice hardly conforms to the New Testament ethic. Like Moses' bill of divorcement (Matthew 19:7–8), some of this civil legislation involves "sufferance for hardness of heart." No doubt this civil legislation also contains some principles binding upon New

Testament believers, but the question of what principles are binding requires argument of a biblico-theological nature. And concerning Exodus 21:22–25, no really decisive argument of this sort has been adduced so far. I maintain that the passage, on my interpretation, conforms to the general scriptural pattern that I have already outlined. If indeed unborn children are objects of God's special providential care, then it is not surprising to find in the Mosaic law a specific, explicit protection for them, and we should assume that *no less* protection than that should be required of New Testament believers. The interpretation I oppose, indeed, also provides a certain protection for the unborn, and in this respect it too is in keeping with the general tone of scriptural teaching on this subject. Yet to suggest, as proponents of this interpretation do, that such minimal protection is the *only* protection that should be accorded the child is to argue unhistorically, to fail to understand the character of Israelite civil legislation as in part an accommodation to the hardness of heart of the people. Thus even if the interpretation we oppose is accepted, its relevance for the determination of our present conduct must be questioned.

I conclude, therefore, that Exodus 21:22–25 does not suggest that the unborn child is anything less than a human person from the point of conception. Any attempt to make the passage teach such a thesis results in insuperable difficulties of exegesis, logic, and application. Since this is the only passage alleged to provide proof of such a thesis, we conclude that there is no scriptural basis for such arguments and that unless better arguments are forthcoming we cannot regard Scripture as even remotely suggesting such a view.

There is no purely scientific proof that the unborn child is anything less than a human person from the point of conception. At the outset, it must be seriously asked whether any narrowly scientific argument could possibly, even in principle, establish whether the unborn child is or is not a human person. The question of whether the unborn child is a human person is essentially the question of whether, from God's point of view, the child has the ontological status entitling him to a full human right to life. The question is religious, metaphysical, and ethical. What mere statement of scientifically verified empirical fact could answer such a question? Does genetic independence confer upon a piece of tissue the right to life? Does physical dependence of one organism upon another deprive the first organism of its right to life? These questions reveal a certain discrepancy between scientific and ethical predications such that no scientifically obtained proposition *in itself* would appear sufficient to establish ontological status and ethical rights. On the other hand, we must affirm that scientific propositions, taken together with the teaching of Scripture, may indeed cast light upon our questions. Scientific information is always valuable in helping the believer to understand his situation and thereby to see the relevance of Scripture to that situation. If, for example, Scripture established quickening as the point at which personal existence begins, then the scientist's skills would be needed in order to determine whether in a given case quickening had actually taken place. But a *purely* scientific argument, an argument containing only scientific premises and no Scripture premises, must be regarded as in principle incapable of resolving this sort of question. Thus it is impossible to prove from scientific premises alone that the unborn child is less than a human person from the point of conception. For that matter, it should also be noted that the contrary proposition is also incapable of such proof.

To be more specific: it cannot be argued on scientific grounds that, for example, "quickening" marks the dividing line between human personhood and lack of human personhood. Quickening is the point (generally 18–20 weeks after conception, with some variation) at which the mother becomes conscious of gross movements of the fetus in the womb. It has generally been regarded as a significant turning point in the development of the child. The heartbeat of the child, however, is detectable at an earlier stage of development, and the onset of quickening is continuous with such earlier "fetal motions." Quickening is not, therefore, the kind of drastic change that could plausibly be equated with the change from nonpersonhood to personhood. Further, it is difficult to see how the medical-scientific concept of "quickening" correlates with the metaphysical-religious concept of "personhood" and the ethical concept of "right to life." Such correlations themselves are not established by scientific evidence, but are rather the result of philosophizing, which the Christian must dismiss as speculative unless confirmed by Scripture. And I have shown that such theories cannot be confirmed by Scripture.

Nor can "viability" be established as such a dividing line,

although this is the point most often seized upon by those wishing to draw the line at some point between conception and birth. Viability is the point at which the fetus is capable of living outside the womb and is generally thought to occur at 28 weeks after conception. This point varies, however, and that variation makes it difficult in some cases to determine whether a fetus is viable or not. Further, the very definition of "viable" may very well change with the improvement of incubation technology. The concept, therefore, does not appear to be clear enough to be workable as a criterion of human personhood and human right to life. But even if the concept were perfectly clear, we would still have the problem of showing why it is viability that determines personhood and right to life.

What of birth itself as the moment at which a fetus becomes a person? It may certainly be argued that birth is a more momentous event in the young life than either quickening or viability. At the moment of birth, the child ceases to be directly dependent upon his mother's body for its own life support. At that moment he becomes independent in a sense in which he was not previously. This fact has led to the suggestion that before birth the child should be regarded as part of his mother's body, and that only after birth should he be regarded as a person in his own right. This suggestion, however, is not a sound one. To allege that dependence for life support is inconsistent with personhood is to engage in speculation. For one thing, it is possible for two persons (e.g., Siamese twins) to share the same life-support systems to some extent without either of them losing his personhood. Further, the dependence of the unborn child upon his mother's body is not a metaphysical or necessary dependence: that is to say, with the advance of medical technology it is possible to imagine an unborn child being transplanted from one womb to another, or raised in an incubator from shortly after conception, or even *conceived* in an artificial womb of some kind, being thus "independent" of his mother from the very beginning. To be sure, such a child could not survive without the care of *someone,* but the same is true of infants after birth. The unborn child's dependence upon his mother, therefore, is not a good argument against his personhood, for it differs only in degree from the dependence of all children upon their adult guardians. Finally, the hypothesis that life-support dependence is inconsistent with personhood is

59

essentially a philosophical supposition (like those mentioned above) with no scriptural basis.

The dividing line between nonpersonhood and personhood has also been drawn at implantation of the fertilized egg in the uterus (about one week after conception), and at the point at which all organ systems are initiated (about four weeks). Some have even argued that personhood begins at some time after birth, on the ground that personhood presupposes some development of cultural consciousness and interpersonal relations. These suggestions suffer the same basic defect as the others we have considered: they fail to show how their metaphysical and ethical conclusions arise out of their scientific premises; and they fail to do this because they fail to recognize the role that Scripture must play in this type of discussion. I therefore conclude that there is no scientific proof that the unborn child is anything less than a human person from the point of conception.

There is also no way to prove, either from Scripture or from science or from some combination of the two, that the unborn child *is* a human person from the point of conception. In the case of attempted demonstrations from scientific premises alone, my present point is established by considerations already set forth. Several arguments of other types have been suggested, however, and in the following paragraphs I shall have to call these attempted demonstrations into question.

We have noted that Scripture often speaks of unborn children in the same language used to refer to those already born. The most striking examples of this usage, perhaps, are Psalm 139:13; Jeremiah 1:5; and Psalm 51:5. As we have seen, in these passages personal pronouns are used to refer to life in the womb—"me," "my," "thou," "thee." From this premise it has been argued that these passages regard the unborn children in question as human persons, and that personhood goes back to conception. Such an argument, however, reads too much into these passages. In the first place, if the fetus were not a person from conception, it is not clear that the writers would have avoided the personal pronouns. In Psalm 139:13 and in Psalm 51:5, David is reflecting on his origins. We have established a "significant personal continuity" between the unborn child and his postnatal existence. Therefore, David, in considering his relation with God, traces it back to his fetal life, back even to his conception. Naturally, he uses the terms "me" and "my"; the use of "it," whether more precise or not, would be jarring, pedantic, and pointless. These pronouns are quite natural even on the supposition that the unborn child is *not* a person from conception, and thus their use does not establish the person-from-conception thesis. In the second place, we have seen that according to Jeremiah 1:5 and other passages the "personal continuity" of a man's life extends in a sense not only back to conception, but even *before* his conception. Personal continuity in this sense extends into eternity, into God's eternal plan. The Lord in Jeremiah 1:5 uses the pronoun "thee" of Jeremiah even *before* his conception. Now no one would argue that Jeremiah was an existing person before his conception simply because such pronouns are used of him. Rather, before his conception, when he existed in God's mind, he was destined to become an existent person. Thus the use of these personal pronouns does not prove that those in the womb are, while in the womb, persons. That use proves only that in God's plan those particular fetuses were (at least) destined to become persons.

Psalm 51:5, however, requires special treatment, for it is sometimes used in a different argument from the one we have just considered. We have seen that this verse traces back to conception, not only David's existence, but even his sin. Surely, it is argued, if David was a sinner from conception, he must have been a person—for you cannot have a person's sin without a person! This is perhaps the strongest scriptural argument in favor of the person-from-conception thesis, and can be very persuasive. Yet a closer look reveals inadequacies. David, after all, is not reflecting upon the origin of his humanity, but upon the origin of his *sin*. And all Reformed theologians have maintained (on the basis of this very verse, along with others!) that in some senses the origin of our sin antedates the origin of our existence as persons. Ultimately, sin has its mysterious origin in the eternal plan of God; proximately, our sin begins with Adam. Adam is the origin of our sin, not only in the sense that he was the first sinner in the human race, but also in the sense that the guilt and penalty of his sin is imputed immediately to every human being save Jesus of Nazareth. But we are not only guilty of Adam's first sin. For Adam's sinful nature is transmitted to his descendants by "natural generation" so that each of us enters the world with a totally depraved nature. Thus "my" sin, my personal sin, the sin for which I am guilty, exists before I do: (1) in the sense that God planned eternally that I would be a sinner, (2) in the sense that Adam's first sin is credited by God to my personal account, and (3) in the sense that Adam's depravity is transmitted to me through natural generation. It is not obvious, therefore, that the origin of David's sin, according to Psalm 51:5, is coincident with the origin of his human personhood. It would have been quite fitting for David—as it is for us—to trace his sinfulness back beyond his individual, personal existence to those events which determined that he would in fact be a sinner. We do not of course suppose that David was sophisticated enough at this stage of redemptive history to have analyzed this situation after the manner of Romans 5. But who can doubt that David may well have had a conviction of the individual's involvement in the depravity of the race? And if indeed David saw his sin as antedating his personal existence in any sense, if such a reading of the verse is even *possible,* then the verse cannot be used to prove that David was a person from conception.

Exodus 21:22–25, interpreted in the way I have urged, has also been used to establish the thesis that the unborn child is a person from conception. I have myself argued that the passage places the unborn child under explicit legal protection against accidental destruction. Since mother and child are under the same protection, some would argue, the child must be there regarded as a human person. We must, however, reject this inference. The passage does not specify how the law of retaliation is to be applied. Is the child to be regarded as a part of its mother, or as a person in his own right? Either way, the *lex talionis* could apply, but it would apply differently in either case. The passage simply does not specify how the unborn child is to be treated under the law, and thus does not prove either that he is, or that he is not, a human person.

We noted earlier that in Luke 1:41, 44, John the Baptist, then still in his mother's womb, is said to have "leaped" in the womb "for joy." Some have regarded this incident as proof that the unborn child is a human person. Yet I am unable to regard this passage as proving that all unborn children are persons from conception. The fact that the child was at least six months past conception (Luke 1:24, 26) and the patently supernatural character of the event forbid us to draw from this passage any conclusions about the personhood of unborn children in general.

Another argument deals with the nature of the Incarnation. The eternal Son of God became incarnate in the event of his conception by the Holy Spirit in the womb of the virgin Mary. Surely, it is argued, he did not cease to be a person at any time during Mary's pregnancy. Therefore we have at least an analogy suggesting that personhood goes back to conception. This analogy, however, breaks down at a crucial point. The incarnation is a unique instance of conception in the sense that the one conceived was already a person before his conception. He was not, of course, a *human* person before conception, but he was a person, and his preexistent personality continues into his incarnate state. (We should recall the Chalcedonian formula at this point: although Christ possessed two natures, he was only one person. The doctrine of the *anhypostasia* of Christ's human nature indicates that Jesus' incarnate personality is essentially that of his preincarnate state.) Since other persons do not antedate their physical existence, we do not have the same reason to suppose that they are persons from conception that we have in the case of Christ.

Another argument from analogy: in I John 3:9, the writer speaks of our spiritual "begetting" by God. (*Gennao* should be translated "beget" rather than "bear" in this verse because of the emphasis on the "seed" that remains in those begotten.) According to that verse, spiritual begetting is itself the explanation for good conduct. One who is begotten of God will not sin. Spiritual life, therefore, begins with spiritual begetting, i.e., with spiritual conception. By analogy, it therefore seems as though physical personhood begins with physical conception. This analogy between spiritual and physical conception, however, also breaks down at the most relevant point. For in the spiritual realm there is no temporal interval between conception and birth; there is no spiritual "gestation period." Thus the spiritual situation analogous to physical reproduction lacks precisely the problematic aspect that we are here concerned to analyze. The argument, therefore, does not furnish an adequate analogy to guide our thinking in this matter.

Finally let us consider an argument that uses premises from both science and Scripture. Scripture teaches that man is a psychophysical unity—that both soul and body are essential to human personhood. Science shows us that man's body begins at conception, because at conception each embryo is endowed with its own unique set of chromosomes. If man's body begins at conception, then man's soul, and hence his personhood, must begin at conception also. The weak link in this argument is the assumed correlation between "chromosomal uniqueness" and "human body." It is natural enough to want to link these two concepts and to suppose that they originate in the same event. Yet it is precisely this correlation that needs to be proved. Can there be human tissue that is chromosomally unique but not a human body (and therefore not a human person)? This is the problem that the argument fails to answer. The difficulty here is, as above, the difficulty of correlating a scientific concept (chromosomal uniqueness) with a metaphysical-religious concept (that demonstrably human body which implies human personhood).

Nevertheless, the Christian is under scriptural obligation to act on the assumption that the unborn child is a person from conception. To clarify this statement, let us review a bit. Our previous discussion seems to leave the Christian in an intolerable situation. On the one hand, there is no proof from Scripture or from science that the unborn child is *not* a person from conception. On the other hand, the contrary thesis, that the child *is* a person from conception, also lacks demonstrative argument. There being no demonstrative proof either way, what is the Christian to do? He must make decisions concerning abortion, and in those decisions he must assume either that the unborn child is a person or that he is not. My position is that although Scripture furnishes no demonstrative proof in this matter, it does show us clearly what our assumptions in such situations must be.

If we begin our considerations from scratch, with no arguments in front of us, we are faced with the following alternatives: either the child is (1) a part of his mother's body, deserving the same protection accorded to other parts of her body, or he is (2) a human person in his own right, deserving the same protection as other persons, or he is (3) somewhere in between, deserving less protection than a human person, but more than a mere part of his mother's body. The first alternative can be dismissed rather easily on the basis of what has already been said. This conclusion is confirmed by the fact that even before fertilization, the female egg is in the process of being rejected

64

by the woman's body. If the egg is fertilized and becomes implanted in the womb, this rejection process is ordinarily suppressed for a nine-month period; but this suppression is only temporary. The mother's body continues to treat the unborn child as a piece of "foreign tissue," as a parasitical organism. The event of birth may be seen as the final "rejection" of this foreign tissue by the mother's body. This relation between mother and fetus does not suggest that the child should be regarded as "part of the mother's body." Furthermore, the genetic uniqueness of the fetus distinguishes the unborn child from all other tissues of his mother's body and determines that the course of his normal development will lead to eventual separation from his mother's body. Thus neither from a theological nor from a medical point of view are we entitled to regard the unborn child as a mere part of his mother's body.

The second alternative can neither be demonstrated nor disproved. Yet its *possibility* (unlike the possibility of (1)) cannot be discounted. The third alternative cannot be demonstrated or disproved either, so we are faced with a wide range of possibilities, the "somewhere" of (3) being indefinite and covering a number of alternatives. In a situation of this sort, the most crucial question becomes the question of burden of proof. Should we treat the unborn child as a human person in the absence of arguments to the contrary, or should we adopt a position in the range of (3) in the absence of any demonstration of (2)? Should we afford the unborn child maximum protection in the absence of arguments for anything less? Or may we take it upon ourselves to give him less than maximum protection on the ground that (2) *may* not be the case? When the issue is placed in such terms, I believe that the Christian will perceive an obligation to adopt (2) as his working assumption, that he will choose to give maximum protection to the unborn child, that he will choose in favor of life, when the issue is a matter of life and death. If there is any genuine possibility that the unborn child is, at any point, a human person made in the image of God, then the Christian cannot assume otherwise, for to do so would be to risk breaking the Sixth Commandment. And the risk is of a special kind. It is not as if there were some evidence tending to legitimate the killing of unborn children (on the ground of their lack of personal human status) and equal evidence tending to call such killing in question. There is nothing in Scripture that even suggests the legitimacy of such killing, and there is much in Scripture which calls it into question. Everything Scripture says on the matter has the force of *protecting* the child, and nothing in Scripture has the force of expressly limiting that protection. If indeed, as I maintain, Scripture does not say expressly how much protection the child deserves, must we not assume that the child should receive maximum protection until someone is able to demonstrate otherwise? Only unscriptural and arbitrary arguments have so far been offered in favor of limiting this protection below the maximum. Therefore I regard maximum protection for the unborn child as a scriptural obligation; and by "maximum" I mean treating the unborn child as a human person.

The same point may be made from a somewhat different perspective. Christians have always opposed infanticide on the ground of the Sixth Commandment. A child, say, five minutes after birth, has always been recognized by Christians as a person in the image of God, deserving of utmost care for the preservation of his life. But what of a child five minutes before birth? The child is not drastically different from the child already born, except that he happens to be still in the womb. He might, in fact, already be living outside the womb if the physician had decided to remove him surgically. The fact that he is in the womb rather than outside seems to be a small matter on which to rest a decision between life and death. Surely this child deserves the same protection, the same respect as the first child we mentioned. But what of a child ten minutes before his birth? Or twenty? Or five days? Or three months? Or six months? At what point do we abandon our high regard for the child's status in the sight of God? At what point do we decide to give him less than maximum protection? Arguments have been offered, to be sure, to the effect that this maximizing of the child's status should begin at some point in the gestation period, but such arguments are far from convincing. And *some* argument is surely needed. An arbitrary decision in a matter of life and death is an impossibility. If someone argues for the destruction of an organism on the premise that it is not a human person, surely he must be obligated to *prove* that premise; he may not claim the right to assume it arbitrarily. In the absence of such argument—that is, in our present situation—the Christian has no choice but to maintain his maximal concern for the young life from conception onward. The Christian, therefore, must *act on the assumption that* the unborn child is a person in the sight

66

of God and therefore under the protection of the Sixth Commandment.

Does this assumption rule out abortion under all circumstances? Not automatically. The Sixth Commandment as interpreted by the rest of Scripture does not forbid all killing of human beings in all situations. Scripture in fact even authorizes the destruction of human life in cases of just war and lawful capital punishment. The question is still open, therefore, as to whether there are special circumstances that would ever justify the destruction of an unborn child, granted the presumption that the child has the same *right* to live as other human beings. A fetus could never, of course, be subject to capital punishment since he could never be legally convicted of a crime. In the wartime situation, the killing of unborn children must be seen in the same category as the killing of other civilians. But other circumstances are sometimes claimed to make abortion necessary. These require special discussion.

The first argument is that abortion is necessary as a form of population control, if we are to avert a crisis of overpopulation. But however great the crisis may appear, and however great may be the desirability of birth control procedures, it is still not clear why this situation ever justifies abortion. There are other methods of combating overpopulation (both through birth control and through economic reorganization), and it is not clear that such methods require abortion as a supplement in order to be effective. In any case, there is no more ground for abortion as a means of population control than there is for infanticide on the same grounds.

Similarly, we must reject the argument that abortion is sometimes necessitated purely by the *economic* situation of a family. The Christian is indeed under obligation to consider the needs of the poor, to sympathize with and help those in economic need. But this does not mean that Christians must accept any and every effort of the poor to improve their economic status. To destroy a child because one is unable to afford the costs of his upbringing would be a heinous sin indeed, and abortion for such reasons must be placed in the same category. The life of a poor child can be exceedingly hard, but many children of poor homes have, by God's grace, overcome their hardships; and who can say that life in poverty is worse than no life at all?

67

A somewhat stronger, or at least more plausible, argument is that abortion is sometimes necessary to guard the psychological health of the mother. So-called "psychiatric indications" for abortion were used, before the 1973 Supreme Court decision, to justify 30 to 50 percent of legal abortions—up to 80 percent in the ten states that had relatively liberal abortion laws. "Psychiatric indications," however, appears to be a catch-all phrase with no clear meaning. Most of those who sought abortions on such grounds were not under the care of a psychiatrist and often had no psychiatrically definable ailment. Further, abortion may very well cause more psychological problems than it eases. Some psychiatrists state that an abortion can lead to more severe mental disturbance, especially if there is some genuine psychological illness present. In general it seems impossible to determine whether an abortion will help or hinder a genuine psychological condition, and many feel that with modern psychological therapies available it makes more medical sense to bring the pregnancy to term in such cases. But what if the situation is complicated by a threat of suicide? Studies show that such threats are not generally carried out and are often manipulative in character. In general, the suicide rate appears to be lower for pregnant women than for other women of childbearing age; the same is true for those who are pregnant out of wedlock. When "psychiatric indications" are weighed against the life of the unborn child, the Christian will regard the certain death of the unborn as a greater tragedy than any of the consequences likely to result from rejecting a plea for abortion on such grounds. The Christian would unhesitatingly deny to a mother the right to kill an already-born infant for such reasons; the case for abortion in this context is no stronger than the case for infanticide, and in some respects is even weaker.

Some maintain that abortion is sometimes necessary to prevent the birth of unwanted children. Evidence indicates, however, that the desires of expectant mothers vacillate considerably and offer little indication of whether the child will be truly wanted or appreciated after he is born. Further, a California study in the early 1970s maintained that 90 percent of battered children resulted from *planned* pregnancies—pregnancies that, as far as anyone could tell, were "wanted" when they began. It appears that since the introduction of the birth control pill, child beating has tripled. Even if a child is in some sense "unwanted" during his childhood, this background need not be an insuperable obstacle to his lifelong—and eternal—happiness. Nor does being "wanted" in childhood guarantee a good life. At any rate, is abortion, death before birth, preferable to an unhappy childhood? I think that this sort of consideration is insufficient to justify abortion. Children that are truly "unwanted" (in a serious sense of that word) at the time of their birth should be put up for adoption. And those concerned about battered children should consider the ugliness of the methods by which unborn children are destroyed in abortions despite their visible struggle for life.

What of the use of abortion to protect the *physical* health of the mother (generally called "therapeutic abortion")? Opinions on when therapeutic abortion is indicated vary greatly: at one hospital one therapeutic abortion per 30 pregnancies was performed, at another, one per 300,000. With such variation, one suspects that other than medical factors enter into some definitions of therapeutic abortion. Many doctors maintain that the progress of medical science has made therapeutic abortion generally unnecessary. As long ago as 1951, R. J. Heffernan, M.D. of Tufts University was quoted as saying, "Anyone who performs a therapeutic abortion is either ignorant of modern medical methods of treating the complications of pregnancy or is unwilling to take time to use them." In this connection it should also be noted that there are certain dangers to the mother in the abortion process itself. The maternal death rate from abortions in Sweden (where again legal abortions are easily obtainable) is 39 per 100,000; in Denmark, 41 per 100,000; in England, 30 per 100,000. These figures from northern Europe are higher than the maternal death rate from all causes in those countries. Abortions performed after the 12th week of pregnancy are significantly more dangerous. In the light of the rarity of genuine indications for therapeutic abortion and the medical dangers inherent in the operation itself, it seems that there are few if any cases in which abortion might legitimately be recommended on medical grounds. When we consider further that even in these rare cases the *possible* physical harm to the mother must be weighed against the *certain* death of the fetus, it is hard to conceive of any justification for abortion on such grounds. As for the extremely rare case in which the very *life* of the woman is jeopardized by her pregnancy, I shall discuss that below.

An argument with considerable emotional force is the alleged necessity of abortion in cases where pregnancy has resulted from rape or incest. Some feel that it is cruel to require a woman to give birth to the child of a rapist. Actually there are extremely few cases of this kind: less than one in 5,000 abortions is performed on such grounds, and that figure includes pregnancies arising from statutory rape as well as, one may assume, some cases where rape has been falsely alleged. In Washington, D. C. *no* documented rape cases resulted in pregnancy over a 20-year period. But what of the rare case where this occurs? Until five days after the occurrence of rape, most hospitals will routinely perform a dilation and curettage operation on the woman to prevent any birth arising from the incident. I am unable to endorse this procedure, because it may very well prevent the implantation of a fertilized egg in the womb and thus effect the destruction of an unborn child. This result, of course, is most unlikely if the operation is performed within a few hours of intercourse: during that period, the operation is a form of contraception rather than a form of abortion. But in view of the uncertainty of timing, I would regard another procedure, an oil douche to prevent fertilization, as preferable from a moral point of view. If, however, neither of these methods is used immediately for some reason and the woman finds out later that she is pregnant, should she seek an abortion? The Christian must reply in the negative. We are here weighing the shame, pain, and inconvenience of the mother against the life of her child, and we have no choice but to decide in favor of the latter. The unborn child must not be put to death for the sin of a parent. A Christian must indeed sympathize with the plight of a woman in such a situation and must be prepared to give counsel, prayer, and other help. In spite of her suffering, she should be helped to see from God's Word what a privilege it is to bring a child into the world, and how the child, even from such an origin, may be one of God's elect—a blessing to God's church and to the world. In some cases, it may be best for the child to be put up for adoption, but in any case, his destruction is not the answer.

Abortion is also frequently recommended to prevent the birth of deformed children. Again, the frequency of such cases is sometimes overestimated. Among pregnancies complicated by rubella or German measles (notorious as a cause of birth defects), only one of four children is born with any deformity, and only 8 percent are born with deformities of a grave character. If a mother's rubella were regarded as adequate ground for abortion, three potentially healthy children would be killed to prevent the birth of each deformed child. From a Christian point of view, such procedures must be rejected decisively. Medical science has made great strides recently in diagnosing and treating deformities both before and after birth. We now have access to Rh and measles vaccines, and fetal blood transfusions and intrauterine surgery (even heart surgery) are also available. After a child has been born with a deformity, he has access to many forms of therapy; new training techniques for brain-injured and retarded children have been developed. This progress seems likely to continue, but the rate of progress will certainly be slowed if abortion to prevent deformity becomes the general procedure. And a still more important consideration is the following: What man has the right to say that life with a handicap—even a serious handicap—is not worth living? There has never been any evidence that people with birth defects are generally any less happy than other people, or less useful to society, let alone less precious in God's sight. The suicide rate among deformed persons is less than that of the general population. In some cases, handicapped workers have been shown to be more efficient and dependable than the non-handicapped. Many people have experienced great joy as well as challenge in the rearing of a retarded child. If, however, we insist in spite of these facts that death is better than a deformed life, what will prevent us from applying that principle to those who are born normally, but subsequently become deformed? And what will prevent us from enlarging our definition of "deformity" as a pretext for eliminating all "undesirables" from society? Eugenic euthanasia, infanticide, geronticide—such are the results of the master-race mentality that is only one or two logical steps from the proposal to kill off the deformed before birth. The decisive consideration, however, is that as Christians we must treat the unborn child as a human person, and that human personhood implies a right to life, even when the quality of that life is hampered by deformity.

The strongest argument in favor of abortion, however, is that it may sometimes be necessary to save the life of the mother. Here it seems to be a question of one life or the other. The Sixth Commandment requires not only that we refrain from killing, but that we make diligent efforts to preserve life. Thus, it is argued, to allow a mother to die without taking available measures to save her is at least as great a sin as killing an unborn child. The question then becomes whether we kill the child to save the mother, or whether we kill the mother (by our inaction) so as not to do harm to the child. This is indeed a difficult moral question, but (I should again point out) one that arises only with extreme rarity, if at all. Many physicians feel that generally it is far less dangerous today to allow a pregnant woman to deliver her baby at term than to perform an abortion, even in the comparative safety of a hospital. Yet no one is prepared to rule out the possibility that some situation may at some time arise wherein the continued existence of the unborn child is inconsistent with the continued life of the mother. From a Christian point of view, the main problem is somewhat as follows: Granted that the Sixth Commandment requires us to make diligent efforts to preserve a life, may those diligent efforts include the taking of another life? Surely we would not wish to argue that stealing or committing adultery or false worship are legitimate when done to preserve life in some sense. The situation we are discussing is not strictly analogous to the case of the father who, when his two children fall out of a boat, must abandon one in order to save the other. The father does not *kill* the child he abandons, but simply leaves him in the hands of God, and such is not the case where an abortion is performed to save a mother's life. Nor is the abortion case strictly analogous to a case in which a man, driving with all proper caution, comes unexpectedly upon a group of jaywalkers and finds that he must steer his car so as to hit the fewest number of them. In that case, the driver may kill, but he does not choose to kill; he chooses only to kill some rather than others. But in the abortion situation, an actual choice to kill is involved. The abortion case under discussion is more like the situation where a person trying to enter a crowded lifeboat must be killed to prevent him from hindering the survival of the others in the boat. This lifeboat case is, however, almost too close an analogy, for it raises the same problem as the abortion case, rather than helping us to resolve it.

Perhaps the closest helpful analogy is the following: A woman walking with her husband in a deserted area is suddenly attacked by an unknown assailant. The assailant is strong, and the husband cannot stop the attack. The husband realizes that merely to wound the assailant may not be sufficient to save the life of his wife, so he picks up a lead pipe, the only available weapon, and delivers a sharp blow to the skull of the attacker. Afterward, he discovers that the assailant had escaped from a mental institution, and thus was, perhaps, of diminished moral responsibility. The husband has intentionally killed a person who could not have been convicted of any crime in order to protect the life of his wife. The moral responsibility of the assailant, or lack of same, was not relevant to his decision. If we are prepared to endorse the husband's action in this situation, on the ground of his God-given responsibility for his wife's safety, then we might be prepared to endorse abortion in cases where the mother's life is jeopardized by pregnancy. Yet even this analogy breaks down at a crucial point, for in the abortion case the husband is under divinely imposed obligation not only to protect his wife, but to protect his child also. Is there reason to suppose that the former responsibility supersedes the latter? Does Exodus 21:15 speak to this issue? At present, I am not prepared to speak to these questions. Some Christians will be able to endorse abortions in such cases with good conscience, and others will not. I am not able at present either to condemn or to endorse the procedure. The question requires further careful study. In general, however, this is the only justification for abortion that I am unable to condemn on Christian grounds.

Granted that abortion in nearly all cases must be regarded as murder, does it follow that the Christian should endeavor to protect the unborn child through *legislation?* I answer in the affirmative.

I do not, of course, maintain that a fully Christian morality should be legally required of every citizen in our pluralistic society. Regeneration cannot be forced upon people by legal constraint. Protection of the lives of persons, however, has always been regarded as a legitimate function of government both in Scripture and in modern legal systems. In American law this protection is not compromised in the interest of freedom of religion. A Jehovah's Witness who refuses to allow a blood transfusion to preserve the life of his child can be compelled to do so. A Christian who holds that unborn children should be regarded as persons should exert his influence upon legislators (and law enforcement officials!) to protect the lives of such persons, and should not turn away from this task for fear of infringing upon the freedom of religion of others.

One objection to strict abortion laws is that they discriminate against the poor, for the rich are able to obtain abortions whatever the law, either by traveling to other countries or by paying substantial sums for a competent, though illegal, abortion here. The fallacious premise of this reasoning, however, is that if rich people are able to do something wrong, the law should make it easy for poor people to do it too. This principle would wreak havoc on all legal structures. If indeed the law prevents only poor people from doing wrong, at least it has accomplished *something* worthwhile. In a more profound sense, the law discriminates against the rich, not the poor, if it fails to protect the children of rich parents and fails adequately to encourage the rich to protect the lives of their children. However, a fair law should indeed be formulated and enforced so as to guard equally against abuse by the poor and by the rich.

Some argue also that strict abortion laws are bad because they are difficult to enforce and are opposed by many in our society. The case of Prohibition is sometimes cited as an analogous law. This principle, however, would remove from our books laws prohibiting racial discrimination, drug addiction, and robberies. Further, granting that Prohibition was as unenforceable as it is often claimed to have been, there is still very little analogy between a law against sipping wine and a law against killing people.

It is also argued that strict abortion laws would cause people to turn to illegal and often incompetent abortionists and hence result in many deaths that liberalized laws prevent. Actually it is very difficult to tell how many illegal abortions were performed before *Roe v. Wade* and how many deaths resulted from them. Some abortion advocates claimed that there were over a million illegal abortions in the United States every year, from which 10,000 maternal deaths resulted. But most advocates of liberalized abortion laws were content to leave quite a bit of leeway in these figures (e.g., "between 200,000 and 1,200,000 abortions")! As for the number of deaths, the figure 10,000 may have been grossly inflated. The medical section of the First International Symposium on Abortion (Washington, D. C., 1967) could verify only 235 maternal deaths resulting from abortion in 1965, and felt that a realistic figure including those unreported would be around 500. The U. S. Public Health Service listed only 130 deaths from both legal and illegal abortion in 1968. Since only 45,000 women of childbearing age die each year from all causes, it would be incredible to imagine as many as 10,000 dying from any single cause. Of those deaths which did occur, it is not clear that the illegality of the operations was the major factor. It has been estimated that 70 percent of all illegal abortions were performed by M.D.s. The inherent dangers of the operation itself seem to have been as large a factor in these deaths, along with the incompetence of some of those performing it. Furthermore, there is evidence from countries with permissive abortion laws that such liberalization does not put an end to the business of incompetent abortionists. In such countries, many women still turn to unqualified abortionists to save money, to avoid red tape, and to maintain secrecy.

I conclude, therefore, that the Christian should regard the unborn child as a human person made in the image of God. Such a regard for the unborn child will involve rejection of abortion, except possibly in order to save the life of the mother. On the basis of this concern, the Christian should use his influence to promote legislation that will protect unborn human life. Adoption of these general principles, however, does not excuse the Christian from undertaking a rigorous examination of the motives of his heart when he makes decisions in these matters, nor does the adoption of these principles automatically justify any act allegedly performed in accord with them. Further, in counseling with those facing difficult decisions in these matters, the Christian must not use his general principles as a way to avoid wrestling with a particular case. The agonies of those contemplating abortion must be shared, entered into, understood, if truly *loving* counsel from the Word of God is to be given.

I believe that unborn children are living creatures in the image of God, given by God as a blessing to their parents. Between conception and birth they are the objects of God's particular providence and care as they are being prepared by God for the responsibilities and privileges of postnatal life. Scripture obligates us to treat unborn children as human persons in all decisions and actions involving them. They should not, therefore, be destroyed by voluntary abortion in the absence of valid medical grounds demonstrating the necessity of such abortion to save the mother's life.

4 The Shadow of Death: Abortion in Historical and Contemporary Perspective

Jeremy C. Jackson

There is a way which seems right to a man, but its end is the way to death.

Proverbs 16:25

"Who is called Sulva? What road does she walk? Why is the womb barren on one side? Where are the cold marriages?" Ransom replied, "Sulva is she whom mortals call the Moon. She walks in the lowest sphere. Half of her orb is turned towards us and shares our curse. On this side the womb is barren and the marriages cold. There dwell an accursed people, full of pride and lust. There when a man takes a maiden in marriage, they do not lie together, but each lies with a cunningly fashioned image of the other, made to move and to be warm by devilish arts, for the real flesh will not please them, they are so dainty *(delicati)* in their dreams of lust. Their real children they fabricate by vile arts in a secret place."

C. S. LEWIS
That Hideous Strength (1945)[1]

But we weigh and grade our vices not according to their nature, but according to our interests.

MONTAIGNE[2]

The less one has thought about abortion, the easier it is to deliver a statement about it. Matters that, while crucial to the subject, are hidden in the closet of unexamined assumptions, are apt to be ignored. A way of opening up this closet is to place the subject in historical perspective. For what, subjectively, is bound up with a hopelessly tangled thread of motives and excuses, too obscure or even too painful to unravel, may assume form and meaning when traced across the broadcloth of history. This, in a sense, is what Jesus did when he delved into the history of Israel to explain the attitude of the religious leaders toward him.

That Jesus assumed continuity and purpose in history, along with their correlate, personal responsibility, is important for the study of abortion. For abortion evokes the question of how man acts in the physical world, including how he treats his own body. And the physical world, the world of nature, is the immediate context of history.

To say that nature is history's immediate context at once reveals a Christian point of view, the same point of view that led our forefathers to distinguish natural history from human history. The strong interest among modern historians in relating human actions to such variables as weather, disease, and food supply is not only an attempt to fill out our understanding of the past. It is also, though not always consciously, a result of the breaking down of this older Christian distinction. If, as we are universally taught, man is a part of nature in the sense that his relative uniqueness is to be explained purely in terms of natural causes, then human history is a department of natural history. It is not surprising that biologists are becoming historians—and historians biologists.[3]

The Christian does not, of course, deny "nature." His body, which is an integral part of his being, receives the same stimuli as rocks, plants, and animals. His mind and soul respond powerfully to the evidence of the senses. What the Christian denies is that his consciousness, his personality, derives from his body. Rather, the body depends upon his consciousness, for the Personal Creator God in whose image man is made was and is a Spirit before ever He made a body. The Christian further insists, therefore, that while his body is a dependent part of his being, he has no right to abuse it because the Christian in his entire being is a dependent creation of God. Here, then, is personal responsibility; and the continuity and purpose of history are related to man's living response to the will of God for His creation.

The bearing of all this upon abortion, which is a radical intervention in creation to take the physical life of a being conceived in God's image, is not far to seek. We may expect to find abortion practiced in societies that see man in purely natural terms. The cutting short of human life is not qualitatively different from the thinning of trees or the drowning of kittens. And although initially, to humor people with scruples, abortionists might join debates on when a baby becomes a human being, in principle this question is irrelevant to them. Reluctance to abort late in pregnancy is first and foremost a health issue, not a moral issue. Furthermore, no one has yet come up with a more satisfactory definition of the beginning of life than conception. The Christian and the biological determinist can agree here that the difference between the embryo and the newborn is one of degree, not kind.

To compare abortion to the drowning of kittens is, then, quite proper. The motive may also be compared: it is essentially born of a desire to control nature. We may therefore expect to find that a mark of a society that sees man in purely natural terms is the urge to control, abortion being simply an advanced stage of this control. Accordingly, the task of the historian bent upon providing an historical perspective on abortion is to trace and explain the genesis and evolution of a "control mentality" in the past.

The first thing to deal with, however, is an apparent contradiction. I have identified the urge to control with the non-Christian, materialist mind. Yet is not the chief complaint of those who have written on ecology, which is so clearly about control, that Christianity—indeed, to be specific, real biblical Christianity—is chiefly responsible for the brutal exploitation of natural resources? Lynn White, John Macquarrie, Joseph Fletcher, and a host of derivative writers have swelled the chorus that under the influence of biblical thinking the West has "subdued the earth" with a vengeance.[4]

What is easiest and most important to insist upon, in response, is that such exploitation is not biblically defensible. James Barr, an expert in Semitics, has noted that the common interpretation of the phrase "subdue the earth" in Genesis 1 is exegetically deficient. The dominion and subjugation are evocative not of high-handed exploitation but of ordered governance appropriate to a being made in God's image.[5] One might counter by saying that what the Christian church understood by these words is more important than what 20th-century scholarship can tell us about them. But Barr goes on to say that orthodox Christianity and recent scholarship are entirely in tune on this point. In fact—and this is most important—the "exploitative" exegesis is a newcomer on the scene. It stems from modern critical study of the Bible, whose naturalistic assumptions led to an emphasis on man's relation to nature at the expense of his relation to God.[6]

It is worth dwelling for a moment on the implications of this last statement. Higher criticism was the research tool of 19th-century religious liberalism, which sought to reconcile Enlightenment humanism with Christianity. The naturalistic assumptions referred to above came, then, directly from a humanism blatantly committed for the first time in the history of the Christian West to the doctrine that nature is god and man is her vicegerent. Thus, Barr can say with excellent reason that

> the great modern exploitation of nature has taken place under the reign of a liberal humanism in which man no longer conceives of himself as being under a creator, and in which therefore his place of dominance in the universe and his right to dispose of nature for his own ends is, unlike the situation in the Bible, unlimited.[7]

We are now in a position to understand some peculiar tensions in the arguments of scholars like Macquarrie and Fletcher. Both of them are thoroughgoing naturalists, but how are they to deal with the ecological results of this naturalism? Quite simply, they correlate—illegitimately, as we have seen—domineering naturalism with orthodox Christianity, and invite our acceptance of a naturalism supposedly in tune with nature, wedded to their own brand of evolutionary Christianity.

Macquarrie speaks of "monarchical" humanism, which he couples with any biblical theology that regards the world as created by God's free will; the world is not, in this scheme, "organic to God," and man is a monarch lording it over nature.[8] By contrast, he welcomes "organic" humanism, which "is much more aware of man's affinity with the world and recognizes that he is part of something much bigger than he has yet understood and to which he owes a responsibility as yet undefined."[9] This humanism accompanies "an organic type of theism" that allows for the idea that "God not only affects the world but is affected by it, even limited by it."[10]

Fletcher, addressing himself to a particular area of ecology—population ecology, with the usual stress on contraception, abortion, and sterilization—pillories historic Christianity as "this old religious naturalism in which human beings are subordinated to the working of blind forces." He goes so far as to term this so-called "religious naturalism" theodicy. Technically, theodicy is the conviction that goodness (or God-ness) is discoverable in everything that is. What Fletcher seems to mean is that Christians mutely accept nature, and natural processes such as human reproduction, as is. He praises, by contrast, "the younger theologians" who are battling the old naturalism "with a new Judeo-Christian or biblical humanism or 'personalism' in which blind or brute nature is subordinated to human freedom and personal responsibility." He continues:

> Decision making is at last coming into its own in the ethics of reproduction. And in this new theology of human freedom God stands behind *men* and their assumption of personal responsibility, rather than behind so-called "nature" and its subhuman cause and effect and fortuitous phenomena.[11]

On the surface, Fletcher and Macquarrie would appear to differ. But it is important to realize that Fletcher's remarks were made in 1966 before he had a chance to adjust to the new vocabulary of the ecology debate a few years later. Close examination shows that Macquarrie and Fletcher's views of man's relation to nature are congruent. Macquarrie speaks of man's stance toward nature as "a responsibility as yet undefined." The lack of definition is the area of man's freedom. Fletcher, equally, does not want his responsibility to be defined. This is what he means when he talks of God's being behind men, not behind nature. "God," of course, only stands for the attribution of value and authority. Thus, he prefers an arrangement that gives man the ultimate options to one that he caricatures as "theodicy," where certain rules are interposed between man and nature, and man and his own body.

What in fact becomes clear from this discussion, and what makes it valuable for our overall examination, is that the issue of man's relation to nature is not a question of "monarchical" versus "organic" attitudes but of authority. Whose authority? Whose control? Whose rules? It is precisely these questions that liberal humanism, theological and secular, likes to avoid, or else turn inside out.

For one thing, refusing to accept a historic Fall leaves the humanist with a purely natural definition of conduct. But the processes of nature are cruel as well as kind. And if man is a part of nature, who is to say that this or that human intervention is "unnatural"? The only answer possible is delivered by fiat, that is to say, by authority. Yesterday abortion was wrong; today it is right. Yesterday the breakdown of the family was regarded with misgiving; today the prophets tell us that it cannot come soon enough. Without a supernatural criterion, who can say which is right?

For another thing, in counterpoint to this latter conundrum, how indeed may one validate authority? In this regard, Fletcher's use of the term *theodicy* is interesting. It happens to derive from a book of the same title published by Leibnitz in 1710, on the eve of the Enlightenment. Leibnitz's basic endeavor was to reconcile Christianity and rationalism, in order to give metaphysical foundations to naturalistic humanism. Without religious support, he realized, such humanism would be blown and buffeted by every passing breeze. In strong opposition to Leibnitz, the main current of the Enlightenment, while not holding to a humanism essentially different from his, insisted upon discovering its own foundations. Peter Gay notes that Voltaire's *Candide* (1759) was a refusal to accept Leibnitz's program. It was "a firm rejection of negotiations on any basis, and hence, in essence, a declaration of war on Christianity."[12]

The importance of this difference between Leibnitz and Voltaire is that Western humanism ever since has rocked back and forth between their positions, alternately seeking and rejecting the clothing of religious sanction. The fundamental tension in Macquarrie's and Fletcher's arguments is exactly here. Their subtly differing formulations of the same opinion are a reflection of their positions on the spectrum from Leibnitz to Voltaire. Macquarrie is a little closer to Leibnitz; Fletcher, to Voltaire. Accordingly, Fletcher's vilification of orthodox Christianity as theodicy is, while crudely in error, historically curious. It reflects an ancient indignation that one must appeal to an external agent for the justification of one's conduct. But more than this, Fletcher's charge is ultimately reflexive: it rebounds upon himself. For, as we noted earlier, he has no external criterion to justify control of reproduction. Therefore, control is no more and no less natural than lack of control. What is, is good. Claiming to be wise, he is in fact the perfect theodicist.

Perhaps now we are ready to glance at the historical articulation and evolution of the positions we have discussed. We shall not naively construct a black-and-white case history. But we shall be attentive to the signs of a control mentality. As I said near the beginning of the chapter, tracing this mentality in the context of a burgeoning naturalism is the prime task if we are to establish an historical perspective on abortion.

While it is easy to see where advocates of the Renaissance as the start of all things new overstate their case, ignoring what is "medieval" and exaggerating what is "modern," it is difficult in the final analysis to deny that the foundations of modern naturalistic humanism are laid at this time.[13] As with many drastic shifts in mentality, which is what, above all, the Renaissance is, what is immediately significant is not so much an obvious change in things done and thought, as in the context of action, the climate of thought.

After all, if one dredges the medieval ocean long enough, one will find not only the theology of Luther but ideas and actions to match anything in Renaissance Florence, in type if not in intensity. Some medievalists have, in fact, done this. But one swallow doesn't make a summer. Neither do many swallows make a summer. A greater underlying change brings out the swallows. This change produced a conglomeration of effects in the late Middle Ages that was novel not so much in its constituent parts as in its constituency. It was, in short, a unified shift in attitude toward the significance and function of man, which may be seen in theology and philosophy, in economic, legal, social, and political arrangements, and in the arts.

The beneficial emphasis of an Aquinas upon the usefulness of human endeavor, in the context of affirming (albeit over-affirming) the positive fact that man and the rest of creation bear God's stamp, had a real-life correlate in the life of the free towns of Europe. Here, the legal emancipation of the burgher from the feudal dependencies of the countryside, and the opportunity within the bounds of urban regulation to pursue a craft and a career to the limits of his ability, naturally engendered a strong sense of personal responsibility.

If most towns in Europe in the late Middle Ages (the 14th and 15th centuries) were losing their independence through the inexorable growth of central authorities, the situation in Italy was different. There was no native monarch, only several private dynasties, to prey upon the centers of commerce. There was, indeed, an emperor but his seat was in Germany and he had never been able to exercise his power for long at such a distance. There was also a pope, but his authority was spiritual, and in so far as this converted locally into political clout it was, to that degree, discredited. In a remarkable way, this special Italian setting mirrored the future structure of Europe as a whole, when the various nations reproduced the sense of integrity and common purpose enjoyed only within the restricted boundaries of a town in the premodern era. It was in this special setting that a marriage took place between thought and action to lend dignity and direction to an existing social situation and an existing ideology of individual significance.

Some of the marks of this marriage, which was celebrated in the rebirth of the portrait and a growing emphasis upon autobiography, may be itemized. There was a trend away from intense clan loyalties toward the immediate concerns of the unitary family. This accompanied a change in the nature of municipal politics, which once vibrated according to the tensions of family name but now favored the virtually absolute rule of one man, at the expense of interlocking family commitments. Accordingly, the original loyalty to the city, which was built upon the participation of many families in rule, was usurped by the new and more remote political arrangements. Needless to say, external facts, such as the threat of local invasion, stimulated this evolution, whose exact chronology differs from place to place.

A theoretical framework for this evolution may be discerned in the pages of Machiavelli, who viewed society as the fount of virtue and sought in its well-being the ultimate standard of value. What links the tight-lipped statism of Machiavelli in the early 16th century with the heroic republicanism of Leonardo Bruni a century before is the intervening breakdown of civic humanism.

It does not require much imagination to see how the experience of the Italian city-state, Florence above all, translates into

the language of the subsequent political and social development of the European nations. At the start, there had been a
positive emphasis upon individual accountability and upon objective evaluation both of ideas and everyday social, economic,
and political practice. This emphasis was thoroughly Christian
and would achieve its apotheosis in the movement we call the
Reformation. But the cancer of self-sufficiency, fed by the
dream of classical renewal and then the nightmare of external
threat, had its effect. Personal and intellectual objectivity came
to be valued in their own right, as a sort of critical absolute, the
function of autonomous mind. And the responsibility for the
control of this critical mentality was vested in the state, as
opposed to the revealed Word of God. Utility was therefore
social utility, what men say they want; not biblical utility, what
accords with the dictates of God.

Thus was foreshadowed the liberal humanism described by
Barr as man's self-emancipation from the authority of the Creator, with its assumption of the right to order nature for man's
own convenience. It is important to stress, however, that this
mentality, with its emphasis on man's structuring his own life,
is only one step on the wrong side of a healthy biblical emphasis
upon personal responsibility. It is the secular version of the
misunderstood spiritual concept of "working out your own sal-
vation with fear and trembling." There can be no such working
out if one is not already, through Christ, a participant in salva-
tion. Carried over into everyday life, this doctrine becomes
"eating the bread of anxious toil," insofar as the Lord has not
built the house.

The generalized manifestation of a control mentality is obvious in many areas from about 1500, as the Renaissance became
a trans-European phenomenon. A detailed, well-informed discussion of some of the practical aspects is given by John U. Nef
in *The Conquest of the Material World*. He remarks in his
preface that "the conquest of the material world has come out
of human efforts never made before, and out of a new hope in
human nature which the future will either destroy or partly
sustain."[14] The ambivalence of the latter part of that sentence,
penned in the 1960s, echoes a similar ambivalence felt by Italian thinkers around 1500. The failure of the Italian experiment
in humanistic control brought on a mood of dark pessimism in
the 16th century.[15] Until the revolution in science in the 17th
century opened the prospect of a new way to conquer reality,

dependent not on imitation of classical models but on the practical implementation of one's own achievements, the philosophic climate was decidedly skeptical.[16]

Whatever may have been the setbacks to the overall movement towards social control, forward motion was maintained. A fascinating companion volume to Nef is Lionel Trilling's *Sincerity and Authenticity,* his Norton Lectures on literature delivered at Harvard, 1969–70. Of particular interest to us is his note upon the word *society,*[17] which bears a connotation, apparent from the 16th century, of autonomy, being, as it were, the abstract noun for a collectivity of individuals. Unlike a term such as *kingdom*, which might otherwise seem equivalent, there is no implication of an authority controlling the individuals.

Here, on one level, is the setting for the political theory of Locke and his followers. And notice that, in so far as we may trace antecedents to Locke both in medieval contract theory and in its revival and refurbishing in 16th-century Protestant political thought, we have the same subtle shift that we have already pointed out. That is, the idea of equal rights, equality before God, and responsible government is fundamentally Christian. But without the overt emphasis upon God's authority vested in magistrates, the slide towards the state as absolute authority, representing all those individual absolutes, the citizens, has commenced. The line is so thin, but it is there. The same line can be drawn for the scientific revolution of the 17th century and for the larger intellectual revolution of which it is a part and, indeed, the prize exhibit.

Objective research, inductive method, the spirit of inquiry— all are legitimately Christian and, as historians have underlined, it is hard to explain them without reference to Christianity. But when they become values in themselves, the line has been crossed. Henceforth, the variety of physical artifacts and phenomena, of human customs and beliefs, suspended under the microscopes of natural and moral scientists, would spawn uncertainty, a sense of the relativity of all things, to minds no longer submissive to the Word who creates. This sense of relativity, which bolstered Pascal's faith in God, was employed by others to rule out a divine absolute, or at least an active, personal divinity. If the social, intellectual, and physical microscopes revealed myriad forms of organization, hitherto undreamed of, then security was sought in the one constant nearest to hand: the mind of the observer. This was the truest legacy of Descartes' putative constant: "I think, therefore I am."

The first impact of the work of the great scientific theoreticians of the 17th century, of Newton above all, was upon a generation of 18th-century humanists. A new hope was born that man's ability to discover the laws of the universe could be applied closer to home: to the economy, agriculture, education, government, religion, human conduct. Not to say that human activity in all these areas had not already felt the bridle of stern human control. Marc Bloch has described the application to rural agriculture of hard-nosed urban business methods, impervious to the traditions of the land.[18] There is C. S. Lewis' tentative but irresistible comment that something went wrong when society began to flout the laws against excessive interest (usury). Apart from his large collection of essays already referred to, Nef has some thoughtful pages on the conquests of the demigod symmetry, discernible, for example, in the evolution of orthography in the 17th century.[19] What came to be known all over as "political arithmetic" had its beginnings, including its title, a few years before 1700.[20] Religion itself had, in many quarters, succumbed to harsh formulaic tendencies of which we remember only hyper-Calvinism. Last, but not least, on the eve of the 18th century we find unmistakeable evidence for the first successful attempts to limit conception artificially.[21]

This last matter deserves closer attention, of course. It is the aspect of control that has as its *reductio ad absurdum* the destruction of life by abortion. This is, take note, the destruction of a life by the life whose self-estimated value is so great that it has declared itself the lord of life. "In my end is my beginning."

It is a *reductio ad absurdum* not in a mere logical sense, nor yet in a simple moral sense, but in the sense that the entire fabric of a mentality developed and nurtured over centuries was implicitly absurd. In other words, abortion only makes clear that what was apparently heroic is actually self-consuming. And, as if deceived, the pioneers and enablers of the latest advance in control, suffering the fate of each successive cohort of the avant-garde, gasp with annoyance when couples begin to use abortion for sex choice. They are thus naively blind to the fact that such an attitude of selfish manipulation is in fact integral to the mentality that had already, long before, selected the tangible and the visible as the kingdom of man's control. As Fletcher candidly expresses it: "I believe with Kant that to will the end is to will the means."[22]

What must be repeated, however, to avoid misunderstanding, is that many elements in the movement of control were Christian and many of the results marked a beneficial and legitimate controlling of the effects of sin, both in the body and in the body politic. But then Christians frequently failed to recognize when their feet were wandering over the line between the darkness refulgent with God's controlling illumination, and the enlightenment kindled by the dream of human self-sufficiency.

To understand the pattern of Christian slippage is, I am convinced, most important. Fundamentally, it was and is a symptom of that spiritual timidity which is lack of faith. It is a declension from the plain teaching of Matthew 6. It is a reluctance to believe, and to practice the belief, that both the physical circumstances of today and time itself are utterly in God's governance. It is a simple refusal to accept that the actual pain required by the spiritual advice of Hebrews 12:12 ("Therefore, lift your drooping hands . . .") can be part of God's plan for us. Surely, we murmur, there is another way. Agag can be spared.

This Christian unfaith bolsters the criticisms of writers like Lynn White that biblical Christianity favors, indeed underpins, all forms of natural exploitation, including slavery. Fletcher, of course, would claim that a further form of this exploitation is the control of our behavior, such as to decimate those "healthy" natural impulses expressed in indiscriminate hetero- and homosexual intercourse. There is, in other words, to this way of thinking, a parallel between the slag-laden industrial landscape and the inner landscape of sexual inhibition. If God has spoken to us, of course, the parallel breaks down, and the claim that natural destruction stems from belief in the biblical God merits Jesus' comment that a kingdom divided against itself cannot stand.

If this was Jesus' retort to the Pharisees, his warning to the disciples was: "Ye cannot serve God and mammon." It is the forlorn attempt to do this, which I categorized above as unfaith, that I most want to grapple with in the context of the evolution of a control mentality, for it becomes understandable and immediate to us when we feel the texture of circumstance. This is why I have stressed that the line is thin between Christian freedom and pagan license. The slow construction of a lifestyle that is sub-Christian in its direction, but comforting to the senses, fools the believer into claiming as his own legitimate baggage what actually belongs to someone else. One thinks of the slow crumpling of the face of the British colonel in *The Bridge over the River Kwai* as it dawns upon him that his efforts to maintain morale have led to a treacherous identification with the will of the enemy.

What is this lifestyle? Ultimately, it is a lifestyle whose benchmark is normalcy. Normalcy means what people think is necessary for well-being. Because the humanist can only accept a span of life extending from birth to death, well-being can only be defined in terms of what is gratifying now. Even the possible approval of posterity seems a hollow reward for sacrifices endured in the present. In this setting, well-being is inevitably identified with the pleasures and the security perceived by the mind and the senses.

Security must be emphasized because the world of humanism is threatening. The Greeks and Romans, as Panofsky once explained when discussing the development of mathematical perspective in Renaissance art, shunned the idea of infinity because the realm of the infinite is precisely a realm beyond the control of finite mind.[23] That early Renaissance humanism, defying its own ultimate logic, was able to postulate an infinite reference point (that is, the pictorial vanishing point) is a tribute to the mixed Christian/classical heritage that is one of its hallmarks. This Christian admixture granted a confidence not finally characteristic of humanism. The Stoic elements would, however, eventually triumph over the Christian as humanists shouldered the results of expelling God from the universe. Lucretius' *De Rerum Natura*[24] replaced the Bible as the textbook of the intelligentsia.

The weight of the universe proved unexpectedly heavy, as Voltaire recognized when, after the Lisbon earthquake of 1755, he railed in despairing anger against the God in whom he did not believe. Again, much of the reactionary taste for neomedieval religious forms after the French Revolution and the Napoleonic era expresses blind fear over the forces apparently unleashed by the mind of the Enlightenment. Botticelli's deliberate return in the 1490s, after the collapse of the Medici's neo-Platonic enlightenment, to medieval religious symbolism seems almost prophetic of this later, more generalized, European phenomenon.

What the Lisbon earthquake represented, to use that as a model problem for the humanist, is the element of chance. In the final analysis, if God is not creator, chance is. The task of the humanist, therefore, is to leave nothing to chance in a world governed by chance. Not Botticelli this time, but a contemporary of his, Machiavelli, had also seen this long before. He had spoken of the need to dam and divert the onrushing flood of fate.

Thus, to come down to earth, the concern for material well-being that, on one level, coincides with genuine Christian concern and responsibility for family and society, is, on another level, profoundly compromising, a sharing of the bread of anxious toil. Christians were and are caught in the toils of this anxiety by systematically defining Christ's teaching in the Sermon on the Mount as the exception, rather than the rule. There may be exceptions to the rule, but the rule itself cannot be an exception.

Likewise, Christians have defended myriad forms of humanistic self-help by misinterpreting I Timothy 5:8.[25] They do not see that failing to provide in this context is not a matter of trying and failing, but of failing to try. It is the latter attitude that the Apostle is denouncing. It is the former circumstance that has always provided one of the legitimate areas in which the church can experience the privilege of that giving which is more blessed than receiving. No wonder, through "editing" its opportunities, the church has lost the secret of real giving.

That Weber and, to a lesser degree, Tawney, were able to identify capitalism with Protestantism (albeit with some twisting of the evidence) testifies to the encroachment of materialistic values. That the republican society of the Netherlands in the 17th century should become a dignified patrician regime that, accordingly, began to reject the work of Rembrandt and a whole school of painters who honored the commonplace, in favor of a pretentious baroque, testifies also to the assimilation by the Christian mind of the hierarchy of humanistic values.

We have underlined that materialistic values are part of a search for comfort and security, and that this search represents a need to control a world that man has declared his own. One cannot, therefore, speak of control in a purely abstract way: it reaches into the everyday physical realm. Neither can one talk about control in a purely physical way: deeds are full of ideas. Tillich's lifestyle accompanied his philosophy.

This is nowhere more evident than in the history of family limitation, to which we can now return. Historians of this phenomenon have documented the close connection between material security or advanced education and the incidence of birth control. Scholars debate whether education, with the resulting exposure to "advanced" ideas, or simple economic considerations, are the greater stimulus to limiting family size.[26] What is beyond dispute is that family limitation is first effectively carried out by the wealthier and better-educated, not the poor and ill-educated. The demographic curve must be plotted socially as well as chronologically. As the Banks point out in their specialized study of one aspect of the debate, it was an investment in a certain high level of consumption on the part of the Victorian middle classes that, with the onset of economic difficulties in the 1870s, led to rigorous family planning.[27]

Not even Geneva can be exempted from this analysis: as early as the 18th century the upper bourgeoisie there was practicing a very effective form of birth control.[28] In this, the Genevans were showing themselves to be no different from their cousins across the border. The practice of family limitation by the French nobility in the 18th century has been demonstrated beyond the shadow of a doubt. With a bow to good taste, the French *bidet,* disguised as a handsome piece of intimate furniture, made its appearance in the mid-1700s. French priests began to complain that couples were becoming reticent about what went on in the bedroom. That the marriage bed should be placed outside the concerns of the priest (and if of the priest, then presumably of God, too) is deeply significant. It points to an arbitrary assertion of human control over life.

We can demonstrate the precocious use of one or another form of artificial birth control by the European upper classes in the 18th century. But this does not mean that they alone were applying the idea of control to physical life. Rather, they above all, having tasted a level of material comfort unknown since antiquity, were determined to guarantee its continuation. There had, in the past, been other ways of responding to this situation. The Venetian ruling class, for instance, to preserve family fortune, harshly determined how many, and which, of its scions could marry. Daughters, in particular, were packed off to nunneries, thereby saving the expense of numerous dowries. This is the general context of Milton's gibe that "nunneries were convenient stowage for their withered daughters."[29] However one looks at it, the Venetians, with the obvious temptation to illicit sexual union produced by their marriage policy, were more concerned to safeguard prestige and comfort than to heed the Apostle Paul's advice on the proper outlet for legitimate passion.

A similar concession to human control, in a rather different context, is discernible in the remarkable evidence, now coming to light, of bridal pregnancy in England and her American colonies from the 16th century. Scrupulous parish-register analysis, based on large samples, shows that about one-fifth of all brides up to 1700, and about two-fifths during the next century, came pregnant to the altar. The apparent reason for this was a degree of individual control, free from parental supervision, which allowed physical intimacy.[30] The back seat of daddy's Ford cannot, then, be an all-sufficient reason for shotgun marriages. The general interest of these findings, though, is that in the populace as a whole there was a steady rejection of biblical principles of control in the area of sexual practice. It was not only the wealthy and sophisticated who were sinning. One might, indeed, offer an axiom that squares with historical and contemporary observation: Sexual license weds sexual barrenness at the altar of sexual control.

But let us return to Geneva for a moment. That the Genevan upper class should have evinced the same control of conception as the French is not surprising when one reflects that Genevan clergy contributed to Diderot's *Encyclopédie,* that "gigantic siege engine trained upon the walls of tradition," as Lord Morley described it. Although Voltaire had his brushes with tradition in Geneva, he was by no means without friends there. The same can be said for nearby Lausanne. In fact, as 18th-century Protestantism became "enlightened,"[31] the structure of older habits of thought and life dissolved. It was not as if the issue was argued, exactly; redundancy is the most persuasive dialectic of all. One can sense the impotent rage of some Christian writers who knew what was happening but could not understand how it had so suddenly come to pass.[32]

We need not be similarly puzzled, for the modern Christian has trodden the same path as his 18th-century predecessors, and for the same reason. What even radical feminists in the mid-19th century attacked as immoral, an assault upon life, 20th-century Christians have embraced with few questions asked. Control of life via control of conception, a battle fought and won for their own convenience by the European upper classes during the Enlightenment, has, after initial hesitation and misgiving, been accepted by the Christian in the wake of its wholesale acceptance by the culture. Addresses to young people approaching the age of marriage, manuals on the subject, private conversations in drawing rooms—and all in a Christian context—assume as a given that one will practice birth control. The overriding concern is technique, and technique alone. To argue against this in Christian circles is about as popular as preaching godly celibacy, and for the same reason. We want sex but we want it without "trouble."

For all that one contributor to an Evangelical publication on birth control could judiciously comment that the biblical burden of proof for family limitation must rest upon those who would limit conception,[33] there was no hint in the contributions of the many other participants that they had either thought through the matter this far or were prepared to make practical application of the principle. Indeed, there was a unanimity about accepting the late 1960s rhetoric of population ecology without the slightest suggestion that this rhetoric concealed considerable gaps both in logic and in fact. It has been left, as in so many other areas, for the secular—or at least non-Evangelical—scholar to discover the inconsistencies.[34] Was the Christian, Evangelical scholar afraid to be out of step? If so, he rejoiced the heart of that early American arch-Deist Elihu Palmer who, in his *Principles of Nature* (1823), looked forward to "a new age, the true millennium" in which, among other things, man would be "the unlimited proprietor of his own person."[35]

Of course, these 20th-century Christians are not Deists. They do not really believe themselves to be "the unlimited proprietors of their own persons"—they belong to Christ, they are bought with a price. But how can one fail to see that, at but one generation removed, they stand unsuspectingly within the stream of control humanism? Even a discerning Christian author, uncompromising in his exposure of the half-truths and downright lies employed by those who have lobbied for abortion, can unwittingly step over the line when it comes to contraception. It cannot be argued, as he does, that contraception is a matter of private conscience whereas abortion is a question of human rights, involving the existence of another human being.[36] Such a distinction between sexual ethics and human rights is biblically indefensible. It is true that in law there may be a distinction between an act involving oneself alone and another act touching a neighbor—although there are exceptions even here, suicide, for example. Biblically, however, one is utterly accountable in both cases at all times. Whether or not contraception is a matter of private conscience, it cannot be argued from a distinction between sexual ethics and human rights.

In any case, let us not decide another man's conscience. Let us not blueprint the order of the Spirit's dealing with another. Let us not upbraid Rees Howells for the extraordinary decision taken with regard to his own offspring. On the other hand, let us be as insistent as we know how on what Montgomery modestly calls the "burden of proof." And if the burden of proof rests squarely upon those who would control the gift of the Author and Giver of life—this life that is a standing rebuke to death and is fit to be redeemed from the curse of death—then we must not be afraid to draw our conclusions from the almost universal suppression of this exegetical fact. It represents a pastoral problem of the first magnitude.

Only now, perhaps, are we fully and finally in a position to look unwaveringly at the historical meaning of abortion. Yet have we not diluted the acid of righteous indignation by raising the issue of contraception? Surely all Christians are agreed in their opposition to abortion, and to argue about contraception is to risk weakening the thrust of a clearly legitimate crusade? But bear this in mind, that the historical evidence indicates that conspicuous consumption, contraception, and abortion are alike symptoms of a master principle: the urge to control life and life's environment. Furthermore, one cannot any longer suppose that all Christians *are* agreed in their opposition to abortion. The evolution toward more and more extreme forms of control has by no means left Christians unscathed, as we have seen.

Take, for example, a reported saying of Dr. Stanley Mooneyham in the August 1976 *World Hunger Bulletin,* which is, incidentally, theologically identical to Joseph Fletcher's sentiments:

The population clock must be slowed. No longer can
every family on earth take as a personal mandate
God's words to the first family: "Be fruitful and multiply." Now God must be saying, "Be sensible and
plan."

Mooneyham is only saying in tabloid style what a participant
at the Evangelical birth control symposium expressed more
discreetly:

. . . the Christian family must determine for itself
whether an additional child might hinder its corporate and individual task to serve God in the world.[37]

The difference between these two theologically identical statements is, however, chilling: the latter was delivered not in the
context of a discussion of contraception, but of abortion and
sterilization.

In case one should suspect too careful a choice of text here,
it is to be noted that not a single argument employed for contraception at the symposium is not also currently employed to
justify abortion. Indeed, to clear away any doubts, the views of
the symposium were expressed in a clause of "A Protestant
Affirmation on the Control of Human Reproduction":

The Christian physician will advise induced abortion
only to safeguard greater values sanctioned by Scripture. These values should include individual health,
family welfare, and social responsibility.[38]

What dread license is offered by "individual health, family
welfare, and social responsibility"? And what leeway is provided by the word "include"? Does the "corporate and individual task to serve God in the world" justify abortion, as Scanzoni
maintained? Are these the scientists of whom the biblical
Christian is so proud when he speaks of the impact of Christianity upon the campus? Who is coopting whom? But we need not,
at least, give way to the impotent rage of the 18th-century
writer. By now we understand.

The tendency for Christians' reasons for contraception and
abortion to match is a function of their underlying desire for
material security. We shall not be surprised to find that this

reflects the long-range historical pattern of society at large. The American experience has been concisely summarized in an article by R. Sauer, "Attitudes to Abortion in America, 1800–1973."[39]

The gradual acceptance of abortion—in practice, in theory, and in law—followed a generation or two behind the earlier acceptance of contraceptive measures. When abortion practice in America became noticeable in the mid-19th century, the laws were tightened to control the evil. The *New York Times* in 1871 showed no signs of the moral laryngitis that has since afflicted its pages. It printed the truth that "thousands of human beings are thus murdered before they have seen the light of the world."[40] Despite the steady increase in the number of abortions, there was yet no attack by pro-abortionists upon current law and ethics. The sense of shame and guilt instilled by Christian culture was, Sauer reckons, still an effective deterrent.[41]

The first real break in the facade came at a predictable time: during the Depression, when the pressures on subsistence provided the base for an open appeal. The future of the pro-abortion movement lay, however, not with the needy. As with contraception, the social and economic leaders of society were in the vanguard. Thus, Kinsey in the 1950s was able to report a ratio of abortions to births of 1:2.5 among the 5,300 white women of high social and economic status whom he studied.[42] This was far above any national average that can be imagined for that time.

By the 1960s, the tension between "anti-abortion norms" and "low-fertility values" had become unbearable; "a normative adjustment" was inevitable.[43] "Anti-abortion norms" means, of course, the law and the ethics it embodied; "low-fertility values" means the drive toward ever greater affluence in the context of the weakening hold of religious convictions.

Not long after, in 1973, the "new abortion ethic was quickly reflected in changes in the law."[44] Sauer wins no prize for prophecy when he informs us that "those holding strong anti-abortion attitudes will continue to diminish in future years."[45] After all, he has the history of the popular—including Christian—acceptance of contraception to draw upon. He recognizes the dynamic of materialism and the lust for security. He sees that whereas Roman Catholic and Protestant leaders in the 19th century strongly opposed abortion, nowadays the opposition from this quarter is, to say the least, muted. Catholics sin quietly; Protestants out loud.

It is time to draw this moral history to a close. One clarification must be offered first, however: where I have spoken of the Christian attitude to contraception in modern times, I have not been ignoring the Roman Catholic prohibition. It is a matter of common knowledge that, if we may assume the reliability of the pollsters, most members of the Roman Catholic community have, apparently, made their peace with the world. The official prohibition stands but, as Fletcher points out, the church's ruling on the so-called "safe period" marked the first formal approval by any Christian body of a method of birth control.[46] This fact, so expressed, is a half-truth, of course. Only by abdicating the exercise of Christian discipline did the leaders of the major Protestant churches allow the pope this unenviable primacy. Furthermore, Fletcher is careless (or careful?) not to mention that, contrary to what many Protestants think and not a few Catholics practice, the rhythm method is not intended as a prescription for normal marital practice. Rather, it is cited as a possible expedient in the same sort of extreme cases where biblical Protestants might think to allow abortion. Nevertheless, Fletcher is right in his main contention: rhythm is just as much a failure of trust as any other form of birth control, if practiced indiscriminately. The same may be said for the refined "sympto-thermal" version of this method as championed, for example, by Ingrid Trobisch in *The Joy of Being a Woman.*[47]

A positive theological statement on this issue is certainly called for and I know of no better brief summing-up than the following phrases of George B. Wilson, which are singularly free of the legalistic naturalism that Protestants usually anticipate in Catholic pronouncements on the subject:

> Theologically, I would define contraception as the use of the human faculty for sexual expression of human personal love in marriage in such a way as to make this expression effectively an absolute value, closed to the intervention of God's invitation to sacrifice, whether that sacrifice take the form of the responsibility for children or the abstaining from sexual intercourse. . . . What must be clear is that for

a Christian ethic such an evaluation [that is, sexual expression as an absolute value] is a contradiction of the rest of the *Christian's* professed view of life, and that this contradiction is indeed the most fundamental reason for its sinfulness. To enter a union which is a human continuation and extension of the union between Christ and the Church, while denying to that union its supernatural tendency to transcend the merely human in openness to Christian sacrifice, is to embrace an impossibility.[48]

The last sentence is effectively and beautifully embroidered in Montgomery's contribution to the Evangelical birth control publication:

Christ did not give himself up to death as an isolated seed; he did it to "bring many sons to glory" (Hebrews 2:10). As the union of Christ and his Church does not exist for its own sake but to bring others to spiritual rebirth, so the marital union is properly fulfilled in natural birth. And since natural birth precedes spiritual birth, as creation precedes redemption (John 3:3–12), so the Christian home can be the greatest single agency for nurture in the twofold sense; thus did the Reformers view it. . . . The burden of proof rests, then, on the couple who wish to restrict the size of their family; to the extent possible and desirable, all Christian couples should seek to "bring many sons unto glory."[49]

First one clarification, now another. The excursus upon contraception, I reemphasize, is an expression not of its special importance but of its having been specially misunderstood. It is neither less nor more important in the evolution and outworking of humanistic control than certain economic attitudes, certain attitudes toward the accumulation and use of knowledge, certain forms of social, political, and even religious organization. But it does need to be understood as a crucial link in a chain leading to abortion and, finally, various forms of euthanasia.

If, as I think proper, Christians determine personally before God whether there might be any reason whatever for them not to welcome the life that is in His gift, they will cease to be guilty of a dangerously relative system of scriptural interpretation that has, not surprisingly, made its inroads in other areas of conduct and church practice. If, by contrast, most Christians maintain the attitude that has marked them for the past generation, they will continue to contribute to a humanistic consensus that recognizes no bounds save social utility. When the objection is here raised that not all social utility need be anti-Christian and surely the Christian is positively responding to the population crisis, two responses are forthcoming.

First, Christian contraception does not spring from the altruism implied in the latter part of that objection—it predates the historical impact of the population debate. Second, just as interested agencies, such as Planned Parenthood and the Population Council, have deliberately loaded the dice in the abortion question to suppress important objections, so has the literature on the population problem been more conspicuous for advocacy than objectivity. It usually presents a slanted picture of the actual nature of the food-resource situation.[50] It implies a degree of reciprocity between nations and peoples that has never existed and could never exist without severe curtailment of personal and group liberties, which only force might achieve. It assumes, in the spirit of Cain's refusal to be his brother's keeper, that the only way in which you can expect a man to help his neighbor is by encouraging a policy of birth control likely to appeal to his personal interests. No doubt this is good psychology for fallen man, especially fallen Western man. But it is not the sort of argument that the line of Seth is supposed to find appealing.

In a more positive vein: as one might expect, the return to a biblically sensitive approach to these matters is likely to have an impact beyond the immediate issues. How could it not be so? If the contraceptive mentality is inextricably bound up with a nervous quest for security, a desire to set unilaterally the limits to one's responsibilities, and an overall habit of cutting to the quick the fingernails of spiritual challenge, then we may anticipate inroads into each sector, both corporately and personally.

There can, I think, be a parallel here to the positive biblical offshoots of the debate over the place of women in the Church. For those prepared to read the Bible straight and act upon it, the benefit of the feminist controversy has been a rediscovery of the crucial place of women in the Christian assembly and the local community. The dullness of the Church in mirroring the secular devaluation of women is the same dullness which has led it to accept the secular mentality on contraception. And just as the logic of this dullness, in pointing toward more obviously unscriptural practices such as women's ordination to the eldership and the priesthood, has led sensitive biblical Christians to return to a more fully orbed obedience to New Testament practice, so one might pray for a similar reversal in the matter of birth control. The shock of abortion, with euthanasia in the wings, might prompt Christians to see in their previous control of conception a natural preparation for the latest developments that must be repudiated.[51]

If a more truly biblical attitude toward women in the Church leads to a great release, or better channeling, of available gifts and energy, the same is true of a more fully biblical attitude toward the family. It is seldom appreciated how much parents are "trained up" in dependence upon God for potential leadership in the church, through having to train up their children in the way that they should go. There is no more exacting school of discipleship. But when parents are carefully limiting their home responsibilities by slavishly restricting conception, they are not thereby guaranteeing a greater and more constructive involvement in the task of child-rearing. Rather, the reverse. The smaller the biological investment in marriage, the more restricted the investment of time and imagination. With Parkinsonian logic, other activities flood in to fill the empty space. Unhappily, but predictably, the same general logic applies to the Church.

It is a fact well enough experienced that the most productive and willing church members are those who are already carrying more than their "fair" share. Why? Because they have come to terms with the needs of the Church; they have been disciplined by ongoing responsibility. They are, therefore, more prepared to give. What is true of the infrastructure of the Church is true of the "building" as a whole. If the Church is made up of families that have selfishly limited their family options, it will, corporately, be a limited enterprise. Whatever may be the internal busyness, with respect to which the observation made earlier infallibly applies, it will tend very strongly to represent an essentially cautious response to the demands of the Gospel. Where comfort and security mark the goals of family life, the goals of the Church will not be far different.

There is also a more subtle pastoral side to this. The life of the congregation should be marked by a reciprocity in which those who have needs receive the help of those gifted and ordained by God to give it. But how many members of the flock go to their elders and deacons with the everyday frustrations of family living and making ends meet? One reason why there are relatively few is that the members, like their elders, have so insulated themselves against disturbance, by resolute family limitation, by a barrier of expensive insurance policies, and by leisure activities that absorb and dull their minds, that when trouble does arise it is not the "healthy" desperation of a family battling the age-old problems by which Christians used to be schooled. Church members no longer seek home help or financial assistance, or special aid at the time of a new baby or a family sickness. Rather, it is a question of esoteric, introverted, convoluted despairs that make it more and more fashionable, but generally futile, for pastors to seek degrees in psychiatric counseling.

Thus, the majority of the flock goes on in its quiet, financially safe way; the minority worries the pastor to death; and by and large, through lack of opportunity, the eldership atrophies without the stimulus of doing its proper work. I am, in short, saying that just as in the "unlimited" family there is much hurly-burly and some inevitable disorder, but much vigorous life, so in a church filled with such families, subject to the timeless laws of spiritual revival and declension. Do we really prefer comfort to life? Our family structures say that we do. It is therefore not surprising that our church structures say the same thing.

In conclusion, let us add to our lengthy clarifications a prediction. Earlier, we spoke of the state as absolute value. Machiavelli, at the end of the Florentine Renaissance, could see no hope of finding one's values except in society and its governance. Reflecting upon the drift of modern 20th-century society, Francis Schaeffer has commented: "If there are no absolutes by which to judge society, then society is absolute."[52] It is fair to say that the more we subscribe to the absolute terms of modern social life, above all its obsession with control, the more we hinder its redemption and hasten its demise. The more we stand upon biblical absolutes, not tendentiously but by faith and in hope and in love, the more we shall stand out. This means discomfort; perhaps the charge of being neanderthal.

But it also means a visible testimony to the Rock on *Whom* we stand.

My specific prediction is that what demographers tell us about the absoluteness of population control in Eastern Europe and Russia will also come to pass in the West. Population control is not just numbers. It is the regulation and payment of labor; the setting of permissible levels of consumption; and the establishment of social and familial arrangements necessary on the parents' side to make ends meet and on the government's side to squeeze the last drop out of the work force. An expert on population policy behind the Iron Curtain writes:

> It was a basic tenet of growth strategy everywhere that income and consumption of households should expand not so much through increase of real incomes of the chief earner (that is, the family head), as through an increase in the number of earners within the family, that is, through the growth of female employment.[53]

Greater provision for women's education and for nursery care was a natural corollary. However, there as in the United States now, the supply of child care never caught up with demand: "As a result, many married women were faced with an option between a child and a job, and chose the latter."[54]

The obvious long-term result of such a trend is disastrous because the age pyramid becomes top-heavy. In economic terms, that means an ever growing nonproductive sector supported by a relatively diminishing workforce. This is Sinbad supporting the Old Man of the Sea, with a vengeance. But in good state-planning fashion, the Marxist regimes responded: More children! In the case of Rumania, a favorite example, unrestricted abortions at $2 each were canceled overnight in 1966. New rules were enforced: no abortions for any women with less than four children, except in special cases; all imports of IUD's and pills discontinued, at least officially. In 12 months flat, the crude birth rate doubled—the swiftest increase in national birth rate known to modern man.[55] Whether to limit or increase family size, the absolute state has at its disposal an arsenal of weapons. They can usually be kept out of sight so long as the people accept the basic value of social absolutism.[56]

In contemplating the advent of similar control in the West,

I am reminded of the old tribute to Hapsburg Austria's dynastic route to power: "Others by war. You, O happy Austria, by marriage!" If the fate of the populations of the Iron Curtain countries has been largely imposed, in the West it is being welcomed with a kiss. After all, the most natural context for the acceptance of the primacy of government control is the dissolution of all competing ties and institutions. Not only is the family breaking down, its downfall is being welcomed. Not only is the economic growth strategy behind the Iron Curtain likely to be applied here to "cure" the malaise of inflation and recession, but the feminists are kindly insisting on employment ahead of time, merely for the principle. Not only would the government's population policy be greatly enhanced by cooperation, but the technology of artificial insemination and cloning, combined with mandatory abortions, might even obviate the need to seek the say-so of the people.

This subject merits a broader treatment than can be given here, however. The thoughtful reader should not fail to study George Gilder's discussion in the closing pages of *Sexual Suicide*.[57] In any case, what should be second nature to the Christian is the understanding that, since man is a unified being, the pattern of his thought and conduct shows a corresponding coherence. The Christian should, therefore, above all men, be able to see the direction of society. It is the non-Christian, disavowing any real meaning to his actions, who is more likely to remain blind to the elaborate web being spun around him. That the web is made up of his own willing decisions delays his reaction to the fact that in the eyes of the state-spider he is only a fly.

The most pertinent Scriptures on control are Matthew 6:27 and Psalm 127:1. In the first text, Jesus asks: "And which of you by being anxious can add one cubit to his span of life [or stature]?" In the second, a simple alternative is presented: "Unless the Lord builds the house, those who build it labor in vain." The last verses of the psalm, taking their cue from the uselessness of humanistic toil, expatiate upon the benefit of trusting the Lord, of having him in control. The psalmist singles out a very significant benefit: children.[58] Why? Because in the long run children are, indeed, only a blessing to the parent who can accept them as God's gift. Otherwise, especially if we are conditioned to think of reproduction as a matter of personal control, they represent severe limitations on our freedom. They make demands upon us that we easily rationalize into excuses for not having any more.

But the call of the people of God is to exercise the faith to receive God's gift of life. What gift of God does *not* require faith to receive it? Having babies will not, of course, revive the Church. Nor will faith, in itself. "The hour is coming when neither on this mountain nor in Jerusalem will you worship the Father"—external propriety is inferior to inward obedience. "What is your life? For you are a mist that appears for a little time and then vanishes. Instead you ought to say, 'If the Lord wills, we shall live and we shall do this or that.' As it is, you boast in your arrogance. All such boasting is evil. Whoever knows what is right to do and fails to do it, for him it is sin" (James 4:14–17).

These words in James are sandwiched between an injunction not to judge one another and a declamation to the comfortable rich on the futility of wealth. We are to live in the middle: neither becoming lawgivers nor lawbreakers. "Be patient, therefore, brethren, until the coming of the Lord" (James 5:7). Meanwhile, in a dead and dying world, it is becoming a more and more remarkable demonstration of the existence and providence of God to raise families and train children in the way that they should go. There is no more radical and constructive critique of abortion than this.

Notes

1. (London: Pan Books, 1960), pp. 166–67.

2. In Marvin Lowenthal, ed., *The Autobiography of Michel de Montaigne* (New York: Vintage, 1935), p. 66.

3. Cf. the biologist C. D. Darlington's *The Evolution of Man and Society* (New York: Simon & Schuster, 1969). Among historians, the French journal *Annales: Economies, Sociétés, Civilisations,* has led the way in the application of biology, sociology, and other disciplines to historical study. Its wide influence and growing acceptance are illustrated in the decision of the Johns Hopkins University Press to bring out annual volumes of translated selections from the *Annales.* Appropriately, the first is entitled *Biology of Man in History* (ed. Robert Forster and Orest Ranum; trans. Elborg Forster and Patricia M. Ranum [Baltimore: Johns Hopkins University Press, 1975]).

4. Lynn White, Jr., "The Historical Roots of Our Ecologic Crisis," *Science,* March 10, 1967, reprinted in David and Eileen Spring, ed., *Ecology and Religion in History* (New York: Harper & Row, 1974), pp. 15–31; John Macquarrie, "Creation and Environment," an inaugural lecture at Oxford University, *The Expository Times,* 83:1 (1971) and reprinted in Spring, ed., *Ecology and Religion,* pp. 32–47; Joseph Fletcher, "The Protestant Churches," in Edward T. Tyler, ed., *Birth Control: A Continuing Controversy* (Springfield, Ill.: C. C. Thomas, 1967), pp. 99–106.

5. James Barr, "Man and Nature: The Ecological Controversy and the Old Testament," *Bulletin of the John Rylands Library,* 55:1 (1972), reprinted in Spring, ed., *Ecology and Religion,* pp. 48–75, esp. 60–65.

6. *Ibid.,* pp. 65, 70–71.

7. *Ibid.,* p. 73.

8. Macquarrie, "Creation and Environment," pp. 38ff.

9. *Ibid.,* p. 47.

10. *Ibid.,* p. 45.

11. Tyler, ed., *Birth Control,* p. 100.

12. Peter Gay, *The Enlightenment: An Interpretation* (New York: Knopf, 1968), p. 203.

13. Cf. Gay's statement that "the Enlightenment was the terminal point of a long process of alienation that had begun centuries before, in the Renaissance" (*ibid.,* p. 255).

14. John U. Nef, *The Conquest of the Material World* (Cleveland: Meridian Books [World], 1967).

15. See, for example, Paul F. Grendler, *Critics of the Italian World 1530–1560* (Madison, Wis.: University of Wisconsin Press, 1969).

16. A standard reference work for this is Richard H. Popkin, *The History of Scepticism form Erasmus to Descartes* (New York: Humanities Press, 1960).

17. Lionel Trilling, *Sincerity and Authenticity* (Cambridge, Mass.: Harvard University Press, 1973), pp. 19ff.

18. Marc Bloch, *French Rural History: An Essay on Its Basic Characteristics,* trans. Janet Sondheimer (Berkeley: University of California Press, 1970), chapters 4–6.

19. John U. Nef, *The Cultural Foundations of Industrial Civilization* (Cambridge: Cambridge University Press 1958), pp. 123–27.

20. Sir William Petty, *Essays in Political Arithmetic* (1682). Commenting on the work of Petty and his contemporary John Graunt, A. R. Hall notes that their "essays in statistical analysis . . . proved that even the hazards of human life were not beyond computation." *The Scientific Revolution, 1500–1800,* 2nd ed. (Boston: Beacon Press, 1966), p. 225.

21. The topic of family limitation in preindustrial times has received a considerable airing in the last two decades, matching the concern of demographers for the situation in our own day. The literature is quite huge but a valuable early study was Hélène Bergues *et al., La prévention des naissances dans la famille* (Paris: Presses Universitaires de France, 1960). The French have done pioneer work in the field and several of the most interesting short contributions have been made available in English in Orest and Patricia Ranum, ed., *Popular Attitudes toward Birth Control in Pre-Industrial France and England*

(New York: Harper & Row, 1972). For an overall treatment that has become something of a classic, see Norman E. Himes, *The Medical History of Contraception* (Baltimore: Johns Hopkins University Press, 1936).

22. Himes, *Medical History of Contraception,* p. 103.

23. Erwin Panofsky, *Early Netherlandish Painting: Its Origins and Character* (Cambridge, Mass.: Harvard University Press, 1964), Vol. I, Introduction, pp. 1–20, especially pp. 9ff.

24. Available in translation as *The Nature of the Universe* (Harmondsworth, England: Penguin Books, 1951). It is fascinating to see how close to Lucretius' sentiments is a biological humanist like Arthur Koestler. His *The Ghost in the Machine* (Chicago: Henry Regnery, 1967) is a mid-20th century updating of Epicurean thought and, as such, considerably less poetic.

25. Merville O. Vincent, for example, uses this verse to justify birth control: "Moral Considerations in Contraception," in Walter O. Spitzer and Carlyle L. Saylor, ed., *Birth Control and the Christian: A Protestant Symposium on the Control of Human Reproduction* (Wheaton, Ill.: Tyndale House, 1969), p. 252. In the context he says: "In this day and age, it is irresponsible for Christians to have unwanted children." *That* is a statement worth dissecting!

26. See, for example: Eva Mueller, "Economic Motives for Family Limitation: A Study Conducted in Taiwan," *Population Studies,* 26:3 (1972), pp. 383–403; also Jerzy Berent, "Causes of Fertility Decline in Eastern Europe and the Soviet Union: Part II—Economic and Social Factors," *Population Studies,* 24:2 (1970), pp. 247–92, where the author finds the economic and social factors to be about the same as in the West: urbanization, education, and female employment. A study of Mormons reveals that it is the college-educated who are more inclined to birth control. D. W. Hastings *et al.,* "Mormonism and Birth Planning: The Discrepancy between Church Authorities' Teaching and Lay Attitudes," *Population Studies,* 26:1 (1972), pp. 19–28.

27. J. A. and Olive Banks, *Feminism and Family Planning in Victorian England* (New York: Schocken Books, 1964).

28. This is one of the necessary conclusions to be drawn from Louis Henry's pioneering study: *Anciennes familles genevoises: Etude démographique XVIè-XXè siècle* (Paris: Presses Universitaires de France, 1956).

106

29. I am indebted for this detail to Dr. James C. Davis of the University of Pennsylvania, who also first suggested to me the importance of the element of control in European life from the Renaissance onwards. The facts about Venetian practice are drawn from his *The Decline of the Venetian Nobility as a Ruling Class* (Baltimore: Johns Hopkins University Press, 1962), pp. 54–74.

30. P. E. Hair, "Bridal Pregnancy in Earlier Rural England Further Examined," *Population Studies,* 24:1 (1970), pp. 59–70.

31. This is not to say that Roman Catholics were not also becoming "enlightened." The main movement of "enlightenment" came, in fact, from Catholic rather than Protestant areas. The difference is that through retaining a strong official discipline, the Catholic church has been able, until recent times, to check the expression of ideas she is not prepared to tolerate.

32. A fair example is the work of the Swiss Vaudois divine Jean-Philippe Dutoit-Membrini, *De l'onanisme* (1782). The title speaks for itself.

33. John Warwick Montgomery, "How to Decide the Birth Control Question," in Spitzer and Saylor, ed., *Birth Control and the Christian,* p. 582. (This article first appeared in *Christianity Today.*)

34. See, for example, the address by Frank W. Notestein on "Zero Population Growth," printed in *Population Index,* 36 (1970), pp. 444–52. This is followed by the comments of three discussants, pp. 444–65. For another example of non-Christians taking a lead in challenging existing ideas and practices, one might select the "natural childbirth" movement. Both empirically and from the point of view of applied Christian ethics, it is hard to defend current childbirth practices. Yet it is left up to doctors and lay people who, as often as not, cite Buddha before Christ, to reclaim this important "territory" from the medical behomoth. To them, humane childbirth becomes a form of religion; to the Christian, it should be an *outworking* of his religion.

35. Cited in Peter Gay, ed., *Deism: An Anthology* (Princeton: Van Nostrand, 1968), p. 189.

36. C. Everett Koop, *The Right To Live, the Right to Die* (Wheaton, Ill.: Tyndale House, 1976), pp. 55–56.

37. John Scanzoni, "A Sociological Perspective on Abortion and Sterilization," in Spitzer and Saylor, ed., *Birth Control and the Christian*, p. 326.

38. Spitzer and Saylor, ed., *Birth Control and the Christian*, p. xxvi.

39. *Population Studies*, 28:1 (1974), pp. 53–67.

40. *Ibid.*, pp. 57–58

41. *Ibid.*, p. 59.

42. *Ibid.*, p. 62.

43. *Ibid.*, p. 65.

44. *Ibid.*

45. *Ibid.*, p. 67.

46. In Spitzer and Saylor, ed., *Birth Control and the Christian*, p. 102.

47. New York: Harper & Row, 1975.

48. George B. Wilson, "Christian Conjugal Morality and Contraception," in Francis X. Quinn, ed., *Population Ethics* (Washington: Corpus Books, 1968), p. 108.

49. In Spitzer and Saylor, ed., *Birth Control and the Christian*, p. 582.

50. See Jean Mayer, "Food and Population: The Wrong Problem?" Daedalus, 93:3 (1964), pp. 830–44. Mayer, incidentally, by no means discounts what he agrees to be the importance of birth control; he simply argues that the alarm over the food supply is totally misplaced and mistaken. His plea for population control is based on the desire to maintain as pleasant an existence as possible. Mayer, of course, is a world-famous nutritionist.

51. It is intriguing that in the Byzantine Empire between about 300 and 600 A.D. there was a significant shift of emphasis away from marriage and procreation within marriage among the cultivated provincial bourgeoisie of Asia Minor. An important influence was a contemporary heretical movement that rejected the hierarchical view of social relations and "the social and religious rules which gave it form." For example, the heretics rejected any distinction between the sexes.

The Church did not, to our knowledge, approve of abortion or contraception, but there was a noticeable lack of praise for children and large families. Evelyne Patlagean, "Birth Control in the Early Byzantine Empire," in Forster and Ranum, ed., *Biology of Man,* pp. 1–22.

52. Francis A. Schaeffer, *How Should We Then Live?* (Old Tappan, N.J.: Fleming H. Revell, 1976), p. 224.

53. Berent, "Causes of Fertility Decline," p. 286.

54. *Ibid.*

55. Michael S. Teitelbaum, "Fertility Effects of the Abolition of Legal Abortion in Rumania," *Population Studies,* 26:3 (1972), pp. 405–17.

56. Acceptance of the dictates of the state, whether actually in the people's interests or not, is almost certainly best accomplished through educational institutions. In this regard, it is instructive to read the comments made by Warren F. Ilchman, "Population Knowledge and Fertility Policies," in Ilchman *et al., Policy Sciences and Population* (Lexington, Mass.: Lexington Books, 1975), pp. 15–63: ". . . it is certainly true that more evidence about differential fertility has been accumulated for education than for any other factor. Most of it suggests a negative influence on fertility. More than that, educational activities are perhaps the most amenable to serve as policy tools, so that the findings of scholars have the potential here of assisting policymakers" (p. 29). It is here, on the level of practical discussion of "policy needs" that we are to look for the shape of things to come, rather than in Daniel Callahan's well-meaning but ultimately ethereal defense of the individual against social utility, *Ethics and Population Limitation* (New York: Key Book Service, 1971), pp. 41–42. Ilchman's comments give substance to Daniel Bell's predictions about the emergence of a knowledge elite linked to government, in his *The Coming of Post-Industrial Society* (New York: Basic Books, 1973).

57. George Gilder, *Sexual Suicide* (New York: Quadrangle, 1973), pp. 251–62.

58. Incidentally, some have taken verse 5 ("quiver full") to mean four children because that is how many arrows there were in a quiver. It should be clear from other passages, however, that it is not number but fullness that is meant. Thus, in I Samuel 2:7 Hannah rejoices that "the barren has borne seven" and we are told in Job that he had seven sons and three daughters. In all three passages, completeness—a completeness determined by God—is central.

It is worth adding here, while on the subject of biblical interpretation, a few words on a common misunderstanding of Genesis 3:16. The KJV translates: "Unto the woman he said, I will greatly multiply thy sorrow and thy conception; in sorrow thou shalt bring forth children . . ." This translation has provided the basis for the popular idea that multiple conception is part of the curse and therefore the control of conception artificially is the same as the medical control of disease, a further result of the Fall. However, commentators on the Hebrew text (e.g., Cassuto, Leupold, E.J. Young) are firm in their insistence that the Hebrew idiom employed in Genesis 3:16 is incorrectly rendered in the KJV. The RSV is here far more accurate in giving: "To the woman he said, I will greatly multiply your pain in childbearing; in pain you shall bring forth children . . ." The stress is upon pain *per se*. There is thus no disjunction between this text and the overwhelming biblical emphasis upon the blessings of God's gift of children to those able to receive such in faith.

5 Legal Aspects of the Right to Life

Harold O. J. Brown

The general question of the right to life, with specific reference to developing life, constitutes one of the most significant issues—social, legal, and moral—facing our nation and perhaps the whole of Western Christendom today. An anecdote may illustrate this. It is the story of the building of Emerson Hall at Harvard to house the philosophy department early in this century. When the construction was almost completed, the president of the college asked his philosophy department what should be put over the door of the hall as a motto. The answer that was given was the famous *homo mensura* quotation from Parmenides: "Man the measure of all things." The members of the philosophy department went off to their various summer watering places such as Walden, and in the fall they returned to find that the sentence that had been graven over the door was, "What is man that thou art mindful of him?" The president of Harvard at the time was a Unitarian, but at least he did understand that there is a vast difference between these two formulations. He wanted to set the tone for the philosophy department as he envisaged it. This story illustrates precisely the point at which we find ourselves in American society today: we face the decision which of these two phrases will be the leitmotiv for our understanding of ourselves and for the kind of society we are going to have. Will we choose, "Man the measure of all things"? Or will it be, "What is man that thou art mindful of him"?

Bible readers know that Psalm 8 describes the creation of man and states that man has been given a particular place in the universe established by God. The psalm places man in the creation order and shows that our fundamental identity is given by the fact that we are creatures of whom God is mindful, for whom He has a purpose. In an interesting little article, "What the Abortion Controversy Is About," Malcolm Muggeridge says that we must make a choice whether we want a society that is essentially run on the ethics of a stock farm or a society in which we understand that we are creatures of God and must in the last analysis be obedient to Him.[1] Muggeridge points out that man is now in a position to decide how many and what kind of individuals shall be born, how long they shall be allowed to live, and "from whom spare parts shall be taken —kidneys, lungs, genitals, brainboxes even—and to whom given. . . . Or we draw back, seeking to understand and fall in with our Creator's purpose for us rather than to pursue our own; in true humility praying, as the founder of our religion and our civilization taught us: Thy will be done." He goes on to say that the abortion controversy and the euthanasia controversy that must surely attend on its heels are essentially asking the question whether man is to be his own god in the universe. "For we can survive energy crises, inflation, wars, revolutions, and insurrections, as they have been survived in the past; but if we transgress against the very basis of our mortal existence, becoming our own gods in our own universe, then we shall surely and deservedly perish from the earth."[2]

Thus Malcolm Muggeridge. Is his warning timely? Is he correct? We certainly are at the crossroads he describes. If we see his warning as correct, it is something we must approach with the utmost seriousness. It presses us to ask this basic question: Does our society need an explicit philosophy or an anthropology in order to function today? Earlier human societies for the most part had no formal or official position on the nature of man. Each had philosophers, of course, who expounded their views. There were lawmakers who attempted to formulate the conditions under which society should live, but there was no fundamental, generally accepted philosophical doctrine of man. A society may even have had an established religion that included an explicit doctrine of man, but in general no such doctrine was imposed by law. In the West it has not been imposed by law even when there has been an established church. We have not tried to remake man, but have simply taken him as he is.

What we have had basically in the Western world since the rise of Christianity is a kind of a broad working consensus, based on the Jewish and Christian Scriptures. Understanding that man is made in the image of God, we held that man has an assured dignity, a definite responsibility, and a particular destiny. One can say that in the West in general this consensus came in with Christianity but coincided with important streams of classical philosophy. This agreement can be seen in two important areas. The philosophical conviction of the simplicity of the First Cause, coming from classical physics, especially as understood by Plato, led to the idea that as there is a single universe, not many universes, there must be a single Cause. From the concept of the single cause came the idea that the single cause was a unique god. Thus an implicit philosophical monotheism came out of classical Greek thought. Sometimes it was explicit, more often implicit. It was in basic harmony with the monotheism of the Jewish and later Christian biblical tradition. Monotheism for the Greeks was cosmological; for the Jews it was ethical. The Greeks reasoned that there must be a unified cause to a unified universe; the Jews, guided by the revelation of the one God, saw a reason for it in the moral principle of universal justice. Justice requires a universal judge whose standards are the same throughout the nations of the earth.[3] These two approaches did harmonize. One of our problems today is that we have lost this orderly worldview. In consequence we find it more difficult to maintain our Christian position in the general culture.

Although earlier societies made no official statement about the nature of man, their law codes reflected fundamental anthropological views. Murder, a crime against the person, was also seen as a crime against God. Quite characteristically in the Old Testament, many of the crucial passages that deal with murder and its punishment view the question from the perspective of man as a being made in the image of God. The destruction of his image is seen an affront to God that can be purged only by the blood of the one who has committed the crime, not by a ransom or *Wergeld* as in old Germanic law, paid to the heirs. Consider first the very well-known passage in Genesis 9, the Noahic Covenant. Another passage of interest is Numbers 35:33: "So shall ye not pollute the land wherein ye are, for blood it defileth the land, and the land cannot be cleansed of the blood that is shed therein, but by the blood of him that shed it." This verse occurs in the context of the legislation permitting a city of refuge to be established for the one who had shed blood inadvertently, or in sudden anger—second-degree murder. It required the slayer not to flee or escape from his city of refuge until certain conditions had been met, because if he did so the unavenged blood would pollute the land.

Law codes on the one hand *reflect* fundamental views. In addition, they reinforce the views of society. The law has an educational value and contributes to forming people's opinions. It is often said that one cannot pass a law that is totally at variance with the wishes of a people. The example of Prohibition is often given. Was the "fact" that Prohibition was at variance with the wishes of the people really the fundamental reason why it proved impossible to enforce? There is reason to think that instead Prohibition did coincide with the wishes of the majority of American people. Otherwise it would have never been adopted. But it turned out to be unenforceable. I venture to suggest that one of the reasons Prohibition was unenforceable was the fact that it did not express any fundamental biblical principle concerning the nature of man and justice. It corresponded to a strong social current, but this was not enough to generate wholehearted support for enforcement. If this is the case, then the question to ask is not so much how the people feel about a proposed law at this moment as how the proposed civil law corresponds to the eternal Law of God and thus to laws engraved in the human heart. But in the long run a law code can do much to influence the views of society even to the point of repudiation of what we may see as fundamental principles of justice. If an act is considered illegal, there will always be some people who nevertheless do it, but a large majority who refrain. If an act is once established as legal, even though not everyone will necessarily proceed to perform it, the natural tendency is for people to grow accustomed to it and eventually to accept it.

In April 1976 the U. S. Supreme Court refused to hear a challenge to a Virginia state statute forbidding certain homosexual practices.[4] It was a rather curious kind of decision, insofar as it implies that the state may legitimately forbid actions that it considers dangerous and disturbing to society. The decision is curious in the light of the Court's earlier abortion decision. Abortion—essentially abortion on demand—was justified on grounds of a woman's right to privacy. One may suppose that most homosexual acts take place under circumstances that are more private than most abortions. In any case it is a bit paradoxical. A privately performed act that has as its immediate consequence the death of what is surely a living being very close to us, a human fetus, is defined as of no legitimate concern for the state, whereas another privately performed act that has no *evident* consequences is forbidden. (If one takes seriously the biblical doctrine of man, homosexual practices are abominable acts that will bring upon themselves a sure judgment, but the Court was concerned only with sociological evidence, which does not demonstrate any immediate harmful consequences.) The Supreme Court decision on homosexuality is to be hailed if for no other reason than that it will tend to moderate the rapid growth of homosexual practice. But it raises the question of logical consistency.

Law codes, then, engender social attitudes. There have been a few attempts today to write laws and to establish constitutions expressing an explicit view of authority, of the nature of man, or of human society. One of the most recent is the new Swedish constitution. Its first article states that all authority is derived from the Swedish people. The interesting thing about this statement is that on the one hand it absolutizes man, or the *Volk,* the people, making it the source of all authority. On the other hand, the statement is completely inoperative. How can the people exercise authority? Through a constant series of plebiscites or referenda? That would be quite unworkable. If we claim to derive all authority from the people, this means in practice that an elite will tell us what the will of the people is.

Our answer to the question, "Does a society need a philosophy or a position on man?" is clearly yes. In accepting a worldview, we must ask ourselves first of all about its presuppositions and second about its implications. The great problem that faces America today is that we are slipping from one old consensus, that of Christianity, to another philosophy that is equally comprehensive and far more oppressive, without recognizing or analyzing what we are doing to ourselves. The presuppositions and the implications of some of the legal transformations that are taking place in America concerning abortion and euthanasia represent a tremendous shift from one consensus, one view of man, to another consensus, another view, which has not really been expressed but is nevertheless pervasive and real. People who would never endorse such a shift endure it because they do not see where it is leading or even that it is taking place.

Let us turn to the question of the agency that creates laws.

Is there a biblical view of the state? Although the term *state* is relatively modern, there is an articulated biblical approach to government and authority, both in Romans 13 and also in Old Testament passages dealing with the establishment of a Jewish society. We see there that the state has a legitimate authority, but that the state is always limited. It is subject in theory and should be in practice to the Word of God and to God Himself. This limitation of the state is exhibited in a number of Old Testament and some New Testament principles. For example, consider the tithe, something that is also under scrutiny by our government. There is now a doctrine that assumes that the money the state calls tax-deductible, and thus leaves untaxed, on the ground that it has been given to religious or to other charitable work, is really a "tax expenditure" on the part of the state. The rationale being used today by Senator Edward Kennedy among others is that since the state is "expending" money by allowing a tax deduction, the state must question whether this expenditure of its money is desirable. There is a certain logic to this position, but ultimately it rests on the presupposition that everything within the territorial limits of the state belongs to the state. Therefore anything that is expended for anything at all is a state expenditure. But this assumes what is really a practical totalitarianism.

There is a clear biblical principle at stake here. It is a principle with which our own society has lived until now, namely, the idea that the first fruits of one's labor belong to the Lord. As a practical matter, we can say in relation to this issue that while it may be correct for the state to tax 90 percent of our income and to do whatever it likes with that 90 percent, it is never correct for the state to tax the tithe, because the first fruits belong to God. At this point the law of man and the law of God are in potential conflict with one another. As Christians, it is our duty to resist the attempt on the part of the state to tax the tithe. In so doing, we act as free citizens resisting the absolutization of state power. This is not our subject, but it is a useful illustration because it shows how we can slide, without recognizing it, into a practical acceptance of the view that the state is absolute. The biblical view is that the state has a *real* authority but a *limited* authority. Let us then return to Malcolm Muggeridge's contention that the abortion issue is the crucial issue for Western society where the state under God is threatened by the state as God. Let us review exactly where we

116

stand in American society. There were two Supreme Court abortion decisions on January 22, 1973, *Roe v. Wade* and *Doe v. Bolton. Roe v. Wade*, a Texas case, is by far the more significant one. *Doe v. Bolton* was rather peripheral. Thus *Roe* v. *Wade* is the one that is generally discussed today. It is not at all accidental that the plaintiffs in the two decisions are anonymous, "Roe" and "Doe." As a matter of fact, the children whose abortions had been sought and denied were subsequently born and therefore living at the time of the decisions. The Courts could have properly held that these cases were moot because the situation for which redress was claimed had already ceased to exist and therefore there was no reason to adjudicate it at all. But the Court decided it did want to adjudicate the issue. Let us look briefly at the decision *Roe v. Wade* and see what it really says. The summary of the Supreme Court decision that one hears most frequently is so false as to be downright dishonest—that it legalized abortion "early in pregnancy." The Supreme Court decision indeed divided pregnancy into three trimesters. During the first trimester, abortion was to be on demand, at the request of a woman to her doctor, without any state legislation. This meant in fact that the state could not even require that abortions be performed in hospitals or under specified medical conditions. In a later decision the Court has repudiated that interpretation, but that it is what it clearly said in *Roe v. Wade*. In the second trimester, which is from the fourth to the sixth months of pregnancy, the state may make such regulations as are reasonably related to maternal health. Here too we clearly have abortion on demand, provided only that the state may require that the abortion be performed under circumstances that will not impair the mother's health.[5] In the third trimester, as the fetus, according to the Supreme Court logic, becomes "capable of meaningful life," the state begins to have what the Court calls "a compelling interest" in this life. From this point on the state may regulate and even proscribe abortions, subject only to the provision that they must always be permitted when the life or the health of the mother is at stake. However, *Roe v. Wade* requires that "health" be understood as including psychological, social, age, and family considerations. Thus we can fairly say—indeed, it has never been disputed for practical purposes—that there is abortion on demand up to the day of birth in the United States.[6] Attempts have been made to prevent such late abortions, including at least two celebrated legal cases—the case of Dr. Leonard Laufe in Pittsburgh late in 1974 and of Dr. Kenneth Edelin in Boston the following year. Dr. Laufe was acquitted, Dr. Edelin convicted. The charge was not the performance of a late abortion, but that a living child delivered by such an abortion was deliberately allowed to die. Dr. Edelin was convicted not of abortion but of manslaughter. His sentence was immediately suspended, so that of course he went right back to work. While appealing his conviction he was named Physician of the Year by the Boston University Medical School graduating class of 1975. I do not know what all this may imply. It may well be that Dr. Edelin, under the law, did not deserve a manslaughter conviction, but did he deserve honor and accolades as a "martyr"?

There were several important things that *Roe v. Wade* did not say. First of all, it made no decision on the humanity of the unborn. It specifically held it to be unnecessary for us, in the present state of medical knowledge, where there are so many differing opinions among doctors, theologians, lawyers, and others, to determine whether or not the unborn child is human, or at what point it becomes human. Now medically such a finding is absurd. There may be a dispute about whether individual life begins at conception or about a week later, at implantation. But all abortions take place *much* later. The Court totally ignored the concept of a right to life. It never asked whether a human being has a right to life. According to testimony by attorney Harriet Pilpel of the American Civil Liberties Union, one constitutional right that we do *not* have is the right to life. In connection with this House testimony on this issue in March, 1976, Pilpel stated that it would be a terrible thing if the government were to establish a constitutional right to life, because then it would imply all sorts of other things. The government would then have to provide food, housing, medical care, pensions, etc.

While all this does not follow as she argues, it *is* true that the Constitution does not explicitly protect the right to life. The right to life was not considered by the Court, although it was fundamental to the quite different abortion decision of the German Supreme Court in February 1976.[7] A second value that was rejected was that of the Oath of Hippocrates. The oath traditionally defined the role of the medical profession, dedicated first of all to doing no harm, as one of explicit refusal to

118

perform or even to counsel an abortion. The grounds on which this ancient oath was rejected by today's Court were first of all that it came from a very narrow sect of Greek thought, and that it was not representative of the best classical opinion. It is not easy to claim that much of what goes on in our government conforms to the best classical opinion. *Roe v. Wade* follows historian Ludwig Edelstein in attributing the origin of the oath to the sect of Pythagoras, which, it says, was not representative. Indeed it was not, because the Pythagoreans were monotheists and did believe, in a way, that man is made in the image of God. Of course the oath had no great impact in the pagan Roman Empire until Christianity began to win out. Then it was accepted because it coincided with the teachings of Christianity. As long as the oath represented a minority view, the Court felt, it need not be accepted because the view was that of the minority. When it became a majority view it was still not authoritative for us, because it was the view of a "sectarian" majority, namely the Christians. This is the thinking that underlies the *Roe v. Wade* decision and quite a few other decisions. If we hold such a view we can guarantee that the one moral code that will never be enforced in the United States is the biblical, because even if a majority of our people support it, it is a "sectarian" view. This was expressly stated in almost as many words by Arthur S. Flemming, chairman of the U.S. Civil Rights Commission, at the House hearings on March 25, 1976. Flemming was challenged by Victor Rosenblum of Northwestern University Law School and clearly did not like his position to be interpreted that way. But that was more or less what it was.

The three values or criteria that the Court did admit are interesting. First was "capability of meaningful life" as a criterion for whether life should be protected. By "meaningful life" the Court apparently meant the ability to survive outside the womb. The Court did not say that only people who have the right education or belong to the right race are capable of meaningful life. However, this language is open to such an interpretation. It uses a very subjective criterion: "meaningfulness." What are the logical implications of this type of criterion? If the right to life depends on the "capability of meaningful life," who is to judge capability and who is to judge meaningfulness? Dr. Bernard Nathanson, one of the founders of the mammoth New York abortion facility, the so-called Center for Reproductive

Health—a nice *1984* name for an abortion clinic—wrote in an interesting paper, "Abortion Reconsidered," that he had recognized after a number of years that he had participated in 60,000 deaths. This was beginning to prey on his mind. Dr. Nathanson wondered how long he would survive in New York City without an artificial aid, his glasses. His question is legitimate. "Capability of meaningful life" apart from artificial aids is something that not many of us could claim, at least at not at all periods of our life. The second major factor, value, or concept is that of "compelling state interest." Where there is no capability of meaningful life, there is no "compelling state interest" in preserving life. It is significant to note here that the state rejects any *subjective* right to life—a right to life assertable by the person who is the "subject" of the right. It only recognizes an objective interest—a compelling interest that may lead the state to protect the right to life. Here again what the Court was saying was very limited; namely, this infant or unborn child, as it is not yet capable of meaningful life, is of no compelling interest to the state. The Court was not extending the concept of "compelling interest" beyond that. Of course it *is* a concept that is capable of almost limitless extension, as we immediately recognize. Does our right to life depend upon the "compelling state interest"?

The third value—and the most decisive one—was the "right to privacy." The Court admitted that it did not know where the right to privacy may be found, but it was sure that it is strong enough to take precedence over any possible right to life of the unborn. The right to privacy is rather limited in other respects, as we all are reminded around April 15 every year; it does not extend to our financial activities but it does seem to extend to *this* activity—the giving and taking of life. Incidentally, the logic used here was extremely far-fetched and went back to a 19th-century decision, *Union Pacific v. Bigelow,* where there was a body search of an individual who was thought to be carrying a bomb. He was found not to be carrying a bomb, and the railroad had to pay damages. This precedent established the right to privacy. It is certainly a very weak parallel to the right of a woman to destroy her unborn child. What should be noted here is that a "formal" right, the right to privacy, has taken precedence over a fundamental right, the right to life. A formal right, the right to privacy, one that is not even clearly established in the Constitution, is thus allowed to abolish the most fundamental right of all—the right to live.

What this also means is that the Constitution is treated as *itself* the source of justice. The Constitution is something that is not expected to be conformable to any external principles of justice, either to God and His Law, or to some kind of natural law. The German Supreme Court, as noted earlier, has dealt with the same question and has answered it in exactly the opposite way. The German decision found that the right to life is such a fundamental right that it cannot be weighed against formal rights, such as what the Germans call the "right of free development of personality," which roughly corresponds to our right to privacy. By any logical ethical analysis, this should be rather obvious: the right to life *is* more fundamental than secondary rights like free speech, privacy, and so on.

What, then, is happening medically? A very quick rundown of the situation is that there were, according to HEW estimates, a minimum of 900,000 abortions in American in 1975. Probably there were many more, because many jurisdictions do not report fully. Seven of ten of these abortions are performed on women having their first child: their first abortion instead of a first child. Eighty-five percent of them are so-called first-trimester abortions, which can be done by the suction technique or by dilation and curettage ("D & C"). These are considered to be the safest of all abortions in that they do not yield immediately evident medical consequences. Fifteen percent are late abortions. HEW does not distinguish among abortions after the third month, so one does not know from the statistics at what point in the following six months the 15 percent took place. If they took place early in the next six months, e.g., in the fourth or fifth month, these abortions killed a child that would almost never survive outside his mother's womb. If they took place late in the sixth month or later, they killed a child that might live outside the womb. Later abortions are performed by something like a cesarean section—called hysterotomy—and produce live babies that might well survive outside the mother's womb. The best estimate we can have on the number of these hysterotomy abortions is from 30,000 to 50,000 per year. When one considers the tremendous furor that is made over gun control on the ground that between 10,000 and 15,000 gun-related deaths occur in this country each year, one must ask oneself why this other extremely high rate of loss of life is not admitted to be something worthy of political discussion and legal regulation.

About 70 percent of abortions are done on women who have

not had a previous child, as noted earlier. In these cases there may be rather serious medical consequences. About one woman in ten who have first-pregnancy abortions will discover she is incapable of bearing a child after that. Ten percent is a very high figure. It can be substantiated by extensive documentation not widely published in the United States.[8] This is rather generally recognized now in Europe, particularly in eastern Europe, where the experience with abortion goes back a long time. The demographic consequences of abortion are obvious. In the United States the number of births fell from its high point of 5 million down to last year's 3,100,000. Planned Parenthood–World Population said there were from 400,000 to 900,000 women who did not get the abortions they "needed" in 1975. Had they gotten them, the number of births would of course have gone down to 2,600,000 or even 2,200,000. One need not be a demographer to understand that such a sharp decline in the number of new human beings born in America will have a rather drastic impact within a few years. The tremors are already being felt. The *New Statesman,* commenting on what Britain has done in this area, said that the abortion wave of the 1960s will be the euthanasia wave of the 1980s. We are discovering a great problem in the funding of pension and social security plans. The conflict will heighten as the baby-boom generation reaches retirement age after living in the age of affluence. The new generation—a selfish generation that grew up permissively—will be few in number and certainly not at all eager to bear the tremendous economic and emotional burden of caring for a much greater number of old people. I think that one can predict with certainty, to the extent that anything can be predicted with certainty in this world, that America's high abortion rate and rapid reproductive decline mean that today's young people will be faced in their own late middle age with severe pressure to set a terminal point for life, to submit to an arbitrary and general euthanasia procedure. It is pretty accurate to say that abortion leads to euthanasia in the short run because of a slippage of medical ethics and in the long run because of demography.

Why should Christians oppose all this? It is clearly stated in Scripture that government under God has the duty to *protect the innocent,* and to *punish the guilty.* Right now it is virtually impossible for a felon to be executed for a capital crime in the United States. A few people have been condemned to death and some may ultimately be executed, but the statistical risk against a background of thousands of murders is very low. However, a child with the misfortune of being conceived in 1978 has one chance in four of being aborted. No matter how one looks at this, whatever moral implications one may consider, evidently there is something seriously wrong with a society in which the biblical mandate to protect the innocent and to punish the guilty has been inverted in this way. A very clear biblical principle states that the shedding of innocent blood pollutes a land. If we are concerned, and legitimately, about the pollution of our country by industrial and other wastes, we must be more concerned about the blood pollution—speaking very graphically—that millionfold abortion brings upon the whole nation. Not just those who are directly involved, but all will suffer the judgment of God. If Christians living in America are really concerned for the physical and temporal well-being of our fellow Americans, one thing is far more important than any particular social welfare program, as desirable as such a program may be. It is the attempt to forestall the divine judgment that we will inevitably incur by continuing to pollute our land with the blood of millions of innocents. Those who question that innocent blood is shed should interview the abortionists—they know.[9]

There is a clear biblical mandate that calls on God's people to protect those who are being wrongly taken to death. Proverbs 24:11–12: "If thou forbear to deliver them that are drawn unto death, and those that are ready to be slain; if thou sayest, Behold, we knew it not, doth not he that pondereth the heart consider it? and he that keepeth thy soul, doth he not know it? and shall not he render to every man according to his works?"

Roe v. Wade not only sheds innocent blood; it confronts us in our American social order with the formal challenge of what amounts to established paganism. Every American Christian should take the trouble to read this Supreme Court decision. It is not long. In addition to the rather explicit rejection of Christianity that I have already mentioned, there is this revealing comment by Justice Blackmun in his majority opinion: "Ancient religion did not bar abortion." The late professor David Louisell, a Roman Catholic who taught law at the University of California at Berkeley, said that this is almost the "perfect challenge." If Christians will not react to this, to such a challenge, to what will they react? As Dr. C. Everett Koop points out, Blackmun has made it abundantly clear that if any religion is to be the guide for public policy in the United States, it is to be paganism. This is not just playing with words—any more than Adolf Hitler was playing with words when he wrote *Mein Kampf*. Note well: this is not to attribute any of Hitler's motivation to the U.S. Supreme Court. But one should be aware of what is actually being said. Often a statement is made and people think, "Of course this is absurd, it couldn't possibly be true." They thought this about *Mein Kampf* and they think it about *Roe v. Wade*. We should not charge Justice Blackmun, nominally a Methodist, with deliberately endorsing paganism over against Christianity. But we can very definitely say that the opinion that he has written *does* in fact do that even though he himself may not be subjectively conscious of it. The result for America will not depend on what Blackmun in his heart of hearts would like American society to be, but upon what he has written in his decision and what it is going to do to American society.

Roe v. Wade has confronted us with the formal challenge of paganism. The Christian in this situation should acknowledge that he is called to bear witness and to proclaim the Word of God. The Word of God contains the Gospel but it also contains Law. The Law of God is necessary for the establishment of a human society in which the Gospel can be heard, in which there will be a measure of justice, and in which there will be the possibility of turning to God. There *is* a Law of God that we may proclaim. It is indeed our duty to proclaim it along with the Gospel.

Martin Luther taught that the Word of God has two parts, Law and Gospel. It is a matter of great importance for the Christian preacher to know when to proclaim the Law and when to preach the Gospel. We are to preach the Gospel to the broken-hearted and the Law to the proud. There is every evidence that we in America today are part of, contributing to, and building up a society that is very largely based on pride, a society that is seeking to become, as Muggeridge says, its own god in the universe. To this society it is our biblical obligation to preach the Law. I would prefer to end on a much more optimistic note, but I think that at this point in America's social, legal, and spiritual history it is important to perceive the matter clearly and say that it is our duty as Christians in late

20th-century America to preach to society the Law of God. We must challenge our fellow Americans not to pollute the land wherein we live: "For blood it defiles the land and the land cannot be cleansed of the blood that is shed therein but by the blood of him that shed it."

Notes

1. *Human Life Review,* 1:3 (1975), pp. 4–6.

2. *Ibid.,* p. 6.

3. Cf. Victor Monod, *Dieu dans l'univers* (Paris: Fischbacher, 1933).

4. *Doe v. Commonwealth's Attorney of Richmond* (1976).

5. Since clearly reaffirmed in *Planned Parenthood v. Danforth* (1976).

6. Cf. C. Everett Koop, M.D., *The Right to Live, The Right to Die* (Wheaton, Ill.: Tyndale, 1976), p. 37.

7. See Harold O. J. Brown, "The German Court's Decision," in *Human Life Review,* 1:3 (1975), pp. 75–85.

8. Cf. Alfred Kotasek, M.D., "Medical Consequences of Induced Abortion," in *Human Life Review,* 2:2 (1976), pp. 118–26.

9. See Magda Denes, "Performing Abortions," in *Commentary,* October 1976, pp. 33–37.

6 The Morality of Abortion
Paul D. Feinberg

In January 1973 two rulings by the Supreme Court
gave doctors an all but absolute right to perform abortions at
the request of the mother. The majority opinion was written by
Justice Harry Blackmun. What is significant about these rulings is that they have had the effect of noticeably secularizing
the abortion debate. Justice Blackmun states that the law cannot favor a Christian viewpoint over a pre-Christian morality.
In his decision Blackmun holds that opposition to abortion (and
suicide) was a minority position in the Roman Empire. Its
emergence as a popular position is coincidental with the rise of
Christianity.[1] Hence, a good many pro-abortionists insist, in
line with Blackmun's thinking, that church leaders should not
seek to impose their theologically rooted views on the public as
a whole, since the Constitution guarantees the separation of
church and state. But not all right-to-lifers claim that the state
should protect unborn life because it is God's creation. It is not
the purpose of this chapter to argue the point. Rather, it should
be clear that with the secularization of the abortion debate, an
ever increasing burden will fall on general ethical or moral
arguments, since they would appear to be theologically neutral. It is therefore the purpose of this chapter to survey critically these distinctively secular arguments and to ascertain
their bearing on the abortion issue.

To this end I will attempt to clarify the question to be discussed in this chapter. Then I will examine the most fundamental and hotly debated issue, the status of the fetus. The arguments offered both pro and con on the matter of personhood
will be discussed. As might be expected, there is little hope that
agreement between pro- and anti-abortionist can be reached.
Therefore, I will explore two groups of auxiliary arguments.

First, I will attempt to evaluate the claim that nonexistent persons can have rights, thus making abortion unacceptable in spite of the fact that it cannot be decisively shown that the fetus is a person. Second, I will examine the other side of the coin: Is it possible to maintain a liberal view on abortion even if the fetus is a person? Finally, some conclusions will be drawn from the discussion.

The Question

Abortion is used in this present discussion to refer to the deliberate removal of, or action that leads to the expulsion of, a fetus from the womb of a human female. This expulsion may be done by another at the request of the mother or through her direct agency. The result is the death of the fetus.[2]

Given this definition, the concern of this chapter is whether abortion is prima facie morally wrong. That is, while there may be exceptional cases (e. g., the life of the mother is threatened), is abortion generally and normally wrong? The issue is not, "Is abortion *universally and unconditionally* wrong?"[3] Nor do I attempt to discuss the question of the removal of a fetus in opposition to the wishes of, or at least without the consent of, the mother where there is some reason to believe that the child, if born, will have severe physical and/or mental deficiencies. Moreover, the matter of moral blameworthiness is not addressed here: while abortion may be morally wrong, there may be reason for *excusing* an agent's action and thus for denying moral blame. It is not that these questions are not important or interesting. However, it is my judgment that they lead away from the central issues that make up the abortion debate.

Thus, the position examined here is that there is *always* a moral obligation not to kill a fetus, and, *unless* there is a greater moral obligation incompatible with the keeping of this obligation not to cause the death of a fetus, it will be morally wrong to have an abortion.

The Fetus: Human Life or Person

Clearly, the central point of contention between pro-abortionists and anti-abortionists has to do with the status of the fetus. If this issue could be decisively resolved, the controversy over abortion would be well on the way to settlement. The main argument against abortion is that from conception the organism is a human being or person, and as such possesses human rights, one of which is the right to life. Abortion of a zygote, then, is the knowing and willful violation of this right. On the other hand, if the zygote is not a person with concomitant rights, abortion does not constitute a violation of any moral imperative.

There are two distinct understandings of what constitutes a person or personhood. Each is supported with its own particular argument, and it is to these arguments that the discussion must now turn.

The anti-abortionist view is that the embryo is endowed with personhood and its attendant rights at the time of conception. In support of this contention a biological or genetic argument is often given. Germain Grisez's argument in *Abortion: The Myths, the Realities, and the Arguments* is typical of what may be called the genetic school of personhood and its approach to the abortion problem. He suggests that the question of the status of the fetus can be answered by responding to a four-part succession of queries. After conception is the fetus (1) alive, (2) human, (3) an individual, and (4) a person?[4]

That the zygote is alive is undoubtedly true. Within a few hours after fertilization it is possible to demonstrate cellular growth. Thus, the often heard assertion that no one can say when life begins needs some consideration. Justice Blackmun makes the assertion this way: "We need not resolve the difficult question of when life begins. When those trained in the respective disciplines of medicine, philosophy, and theology are unable to arrive at any consensus, the judiciary, at this point in the development of man's knowledge, is not in a position to speculate as to the answer."[5] This statement is puzzling. Since there is no question in the minds of biologists and embryologists that the embryo is alive, what Blackmun and others must mean when they make such statements is that no one can tell when a human life or personhood begins.[6]

Not only is the embryo alive, but anti-abortionists think that the evidence favors the position that it is human. For them humanity is defined in terms of genetic structure. At conception the embryo receives his or her DNA strands or genetic code. These codes are species-specific and remain so throughout life. The zygote is therefore human.[7]

In support of the humanity of the embryo Grisez also invokes the Aristotelian theory of substantial change.[8] Before fertilization, both the egg and the sperm can be understood as belonging to the one from whom they are derived. However, once conception has taken place, a new cell exists. It cannot be identified with either of the parents. In the union a *distinct* entity is produced. Furthermore, Grisez argues that the unity of the new ovum is continuous with what develops from it. Or to put it another way, the facts of genetics support the contention that there is a substantial identity between the fertilized egg, the viable fetus, the infant, the child, and the adult.[9]

If the argument has been convincing to this point, then it seems that a new and unique individual has been formed at conception. Grisez can claim that "the proper demarcation between parents and offspring is conception, and so the new individual begins with conception. From this point of view, then, it is certain that the embryo from conception until birth is a living, human, individual."[10]

The conclusion drawn from all of this is that an embryo or fetus that can be shown to be a living, human individual should also be considered a person and granted appropriate rights, one of which is the right to life.

While the evidence just presented is indeed formidable, it has been attacked by pro-abortionists at all but the first point. Is the fetus human? The genetic or biological argument rests humanity on DNA strands or the genetic code. However, such a structural criterion is rooted in *chemical* values only. This is certainly a possible but arguably a shaky foundation for locating the varied *human* values that society has traditionally revered. One might argue that genetic structure is a necessary condition of being human, but not a sufficient one.

Furthermore, recent advances in genetics raise an interesting question. Would, or maybe better, *should* artifically generated fetuses be granted the same humanity and rights that naturally generated fetuses are accorded? Intuitively, the response seems to be no. Yet the artifically conceived embryos meet the same genetic criterion as do their natural counterparts. It seems arbitrary to deny them human status. Or perhaps the criteria are incomplete.

Another argument used against the humanity of the fetus has been called "the morphological argument." The early fetal form, it is claimed, is not human but passes through plantlike, wormlike, fishlike, and animal-like stages before finally reaching the human stage. This argument is dubious at best since it is concerned almost entirely with passing, external characteristics like so-called tails and gill slits, while almost entirely ignoring the enduring features such as the genetic code and the continuity of development in the embryo.[11]

Finally, the pro-abortionist might agree that human life indeed does begin at conception, but disagree about the significance that should be placed upon this fact. Callahan put it well: "While the genetic and developmental school agree that individual human life begins at conception, they disagree about whether full value ought to be assigned at once to the life thus begun."[12] The reason for withholding full value will become evident in the discussion that is to follow about personhood.

The individuality of the fetus is also called into question. It is hard to overcome the initial idea of the metaphysical and physical dependence of the child on the mother. There does seem to be some plausibility to the claim that the embryo is a "growth" in or a "part" of the mother's body.

A second objection to the claim that the embryo is a unique individual from conception is derived from the fact that so many pregnancies (an estimated 20 to 30 percent) result in spontaneous abortion. Since a human individual is believed to have a soul, spontaneous abortions would represent a large percentage of these souls never being born. This objection rests on two dubious assumptions. The first is that there can be no person where there is a large number of deaths, and second that 20 to 30 percent mortality is a large portion. It should be noted that throughout most of the history of humanity 70 percent of the babies born died in infancy.

By far the most formidable objection relates to twinning and mosaics. It may be a bit hasty, some object, to claim that a unique human being is produced at conception since twinning occurs later in the development of the embryo. Twinning involves the splitting of the zygote into two zygotes. This usually takes place between the seventh and fourteenth day. Since it is hard to see how one person can split into two persons, Ramsey has called this problem of segmentation the "rebuttal argument" to the genetic school.[13] If one were to ask the parents of identical twins when the individual lives of each began, in the light of modern genetics they would not likely say before segmentation.

Joseph T. Mangan, S. J. seeks to answer this objection by an appeal to mystery. He says that "it would be a disservice to exaggerate the importance of precisely how our heavenly Father brings about the animation of the two persons who develop as identical twins. That is a mystery."[14] At the same time he holds firmly to immediate animation. Twinning is only allowed to introduce a modest revision of his position. He contends that "the identical-twin difficulty is hardly decisive in determining that hominization occurs after conception, except in the case of one of the identical twins."[15] Mangan thus allows "mediate animation" or "delayed hominization" in the case of the twins, although it cannot be known which one.

On this matter, Grisez says that the two individuals may begin to be present before segmentation is observable. He cites the possibility that a genetic factor is established at conception that will lead to twinning. His views, however, become less convincing as one examines his response to the apparent scientific fact that the duality that will later result in the formation of twins is not present at an earlier stage in the zygote. He suggests that the zygote and blastocyst, until the 7 to 14 days in which twinning can occur, are an individual distinct from the parents. Further, the twins are individuals distinct from one another *and* from that 7-to-14-day-old individual from which they came. Grisez takes up with apparent seriousness the possibility that "we should think of identical twins as *grandchildren* of their putative parents, the individual that divided being the true offspring, and the identical twins children of the offspring by atypical reproduction."[16]

There is, however, an even more perplexing problem connected with the discussion at hand. It is the problem of mosaics. Not only may one fertilized ovum become two individuals, but two fertilized eggs may become one individual. What may be called a fluidity or indeterminacy in either direction persists during the first few days of life. For this reason, Ramsey holds that it is not until after blastocyst that one has an individual human life.[17]

Now the supporters of the genetic school of thought might accept Ramsey's modification, and claim that such a modification is really of no consequence since most women are not even aware of the fact that they are pregnant during the first couple of weeks of a pregnancy. However, such a concession does allow for eventualities that are clearly unacceptable to the anti-abortionist. For instance, abortive mechanisms like intrauterine devices would be permissible, as would the "morning after" pill.[18]

By far the hardest of the four points to establish is that the fetus is a person. The pro-abortionist will not accept the view that human life and personhood are coterminous. In both philosophy and psychology personhood is related to specific rational, social, and emotional functions that the fetus does not and cannot exhibit.

Engelhardt attempts in an unusual way to demonstrate that the fetus is not a person. He accepts Wittgenstein's remarks to the effect that "essence is expressed by grammar"[19] and that "the grammar tells us what kind of object anything is."[20] The question of personhood does not reduce to merely a question of language but language gives us some idea of ontology. Having laid down these ground rules, he argues that the pronouns "he" or "she" cannot be used of a fetus *in utero* since neither sex roles nor personal roles can be played. Moreover, it is nonsensical to ask of a fetus, "What were you doing before birth?" From this Engelhardt concludes that linguistic usage supports the contention that the fetus is not a personal being.

Upon reflection, however, Engelhardt's argument becomes less convincing. Do parents seldom use "he" or "she" for the embryo because they believe it has no personal or sex role to play, or because they have no idea of the sex of the unborn child? If techniques now being tested do make it possible to determine accurately the sex of a child from the time of conception or shortly thereafter, would not parents use personal pronouns in referring to the fetus? It is even conceivable that they might name the child before birth. With respect to questioning the fetus on what he or she had done before birth, the difficulty arises not because the question makes no sense but because the fetus has no remembrance of what happened. It is known that the embryo does certain things like suck his or her thumb and kick (ask any mother for verification). Language is thus no indicator of personhood or lack of it *in utero*.

Because of these problems, a number of theologians and ethicists have tried to develop an anti-abortion argument in terms of potential personhood. Rather than defending the claim that the fetus is a human person from conception, they contend that the embryo is at least potentially human and as such deserves protection.[21] R. M. Hare has proposed just such an argument.

He thinks that the question between pro-abortionist and anti-abortionist should be phrased in this way: Is there anything in the fetus or the person it will become that makes killing it immoral?[22] The most important thing about the fetus that raises moral questions is that, if not terminated, the pregnancy will eventuate in the birth and growth to maturity of a person just like presently living adults. Hare recognizes that "the word *person* here reenters the argument, but in a context and with meaning that does not give rise to the old troubles.[23] It is the "potentiality" that the fetus has of becoming a person in the full ordinary sense of that term that causes the difficulties.

The root of the difficulty can be explained by Hare's reference to the Golden Rule, which is the formal basis of most moral reasoning. This teaches that one should do to others what he is glad was done to him. The importance of this rule for the question of abortion may be put as follows. "If we are glad that nobody terminated the pregnancy that resulted in *our* birth, then we are enjoined not, *ceteris paribus,* to terminate any pregnancy which will result in the birth of a person having a life like ours."[24]

Immediately, it appears that if a woman is unhappy with her own life, she would be justified in aborting the fetus. Not entirely so, says Hare. "Those who are not glad they were born will still have a reason for not aborting those who would be glad; for even the former wish that, if they had been going to be glad they were born, nobody should have aborted them."[25]

Thus, Hare puts this in terms of a potentiality principle that says, "If it would be wrong to kill an adult human being because he has certain properties, it is wrong to kill an organism (e.g., a fetus) that will come to have that property if it develops normally."[26] Further, Hare says that in applying the potentiality principle consideration should be given to all potential beings involved (e.g., the children who may be born after this child).

The questions that such a position raises are multiple. First, the move to potential persons clearly relaxes the moral prohibition against abortion. Killing potential persons is not nearly as reprehensible as killing actual people. With respect to Hare's approach, while it is true that a woman can decide against abortion even if she is unhappy with her life, an abortion can nevertheless be justified on these grounds. This gives the mother almost divine powers in a situation where she is hardly disinterested. There is also the problem of calculation. How many potential persons and how distant (grandchildren, great-grandchildren, etc.) are to count in the calculation? Further, the greater the number, the more likely one is to be mistaken in calculating. And the talk of potential persons raises the whole issue of value. Is human value to be located in the potential for certain properties, or is the value in the actual possession of these properties? If the latter, it will be admissible to abort a fetus since it does not now and will not if aborted possess them. While this may seem unacceptable to the anti-abortionist, it is nevertheless the contention of the pro-abortionist that one must be able to distinguish between present and future value.[27]

The point I am making is that there is no reason to demand that someone who will one day be a person *must* be treated as one now. For instance, little Johnny has no right to demand that, because he will become Mary's husband someday, she must treat him as her husband now. Atkinson is right when he says, "The only way in which appeal to the potential personhood of the embryo can be relevant is by treating it as a remarkably unperspicuous, shorthand form of the argument being presented here: that no relevant moral distinction can be drawn between killing the unborn and born."[28] Finally, does it make any sense to speak of the rights of potential persons? Is it not actual people who have rights? Mary Anne Warren reflects this general attitude: "But even if a potential person does have some prima facie right to life, such a right could not possibly outweigh the right of a woman to obtain an abortion, since the rights of any actual person invariably outweigh those of any potential person, whenever the two conflict."[29]

The major alternative to a genetic or structural approach to personhood is a developmental view. The argument here is primarily social. Fundamental to this position is the belief that human value is "an achievement rather than an endowment." Some adherents of this developmental school would agree that human life begins at conception; others would not. However, they are in agreement that human value or personhood does *not* begin at conception. Value is achieved in social interaction. A fetus is a human being, a member of the biological species *homo sapiens,* but is not a person who is said to be "a fully fledged member of a human community, someone having a developed concept of *self,* memories, a language, and/or moral obligations as well as moral rights . . ."[30]

Mary Anne Warren suggests five traits or criteria that are

most central to the idea of personhood. They are roughly the following: (1) consciousness of things external and internal to oneself, and especially the ability to feel pain; (2) reasoning; (3) self-motivated activity, activity that is independent of genetic or external control; (4) the ability to communicate with an indefinite number of contents and topics; and (5) the presence of self-concepts and self-awareness.

It is clear from the above criteria that a fetus does not and cannot exhibit these traits. Hence, the fetus should not be considered a person. Since only persons can be members of moral communities and thus possess rights, the embryo has no rights and can at the wish of the mother be aborted.[31]

There are, however, a number of serious objections to a developmental or sociological interpretation of personhood and value. It should be noted, to begin with, that this view does not arise from an attempt to choose from existing possibilities as to the beginning of human life, or from an effort to synthesize the truth contained in previous positions. Rather it is a new invention that *omits* the primary claim made by each and every previous attempt to draw the line on life's beginning. The constant was that wherever life was determined to begin, at that point also began the dignity and sanctity of human life and the concomitant moral claim to equal respect and equal protection. Ramsey points out that while Christian teaching and common law have changed their views about abortion, the change has always been in line with beliefs about the commencement of life so that "the unnecessary destruction of a fetus after quickening was a form of homicide." This new approach proposes "that developmental value can be ascribed to human life in separation from the question of the beginning of the life, and that the evaluations upon admitted lives accepted into our 'moral policy' can be unequal and relative."[32]

At the heart of this view of personhood is a definition of personhood and value that is primarily stipulative in nature. To accept such a definition is particularly dangerous since there are alternatives that grant personhood to the fetus or at least take a more moderate view. One can vividly see the danger in an uncritical acceptance of this definition since one can, and some have, so defined value as to exclude Jews, Blacks, Asians, and American Indians.[33]

By far the most serious objection to this argument is that if

136

it proves anything it proves too much. It is an example of what is called a "slippery slope" argument, because the same argument could be used to support infanticide and euthanasia. If personhood and human value depend upon certain achievements like reasoning and the ability to communicate, then infants, as well as those who can never achieve these functions or have lost them, can be killed. Now it might be argued by adherents of this position that one can and does draw the line at birth. Birth confers moral rights on the individual. Unless a good reason can be given for conferring these rights at birth, however, the view is arbitrary. At least a plausible answer might be that the fetus is now independent. But this is simply false. A newborn baby is no more independent immediately after birth than before, since he would die within a few hours if not properly cared for. The newborn is totally dependent. Nevertheless, he is independent of his mother. This is partially but not entirely true, since there are children somewhere in the world who will die because their mothers die or are too sick to care for them properly.

In light of the argument just advanced, suppose the pro-abortionist were to extend protection and rights to babies that could live if separated from their mothers—viable fetuses—but no further. Can a good reason be given for such a decision? Again, it would seem that the reason would have to be that the child can live independently of the mother. In response to this one can point to the expectation that the embryo of the future will be potentially independent of its mother at every stage of its development. Embryos could be created artifically to live independently of any mother, and naturally generated embryos could be saved at any stage of growth should their mothers die. The fact that this is a future development is irrelevant to the discussion since those who advocate abortion will not change their views on the day that embryos can be grown outside the womb. They are not saying, "Get your abortions now since advancing technology is going to make them immoral."[34]

Someone might counter that the picture I have painted omitted one relevant piece of information. Those artificially generated embryos will depend on machines for their continued existence. Therefore, they cannot be considered viable. If this is so, the argument has come full circle, since there are some babies already born who must live with heart, lung, or kidney machines. Thus, any reason for killing the artificial but savable embryos will be a good reason for killing some infants. No relevant distinction can be made between the zygote and the later stages of development so as to justify drawing the line anywhere but at conception.

Norman Gillespie has attempted to answer the line-drawing problem by pointing to the fact that the nonmoral properties (e.g., viability, brain activity, independence, memory, etc.) have an important comparative element. "Even if someone does not know on what basis we say that adult human beings have rights, he can appreciate that children are sufficiently like adults to have some rights, that the same is true of small children, that about-to-be-born babies are comparatively like infants, and that fetuses are comparatively similar to about-to-be-born babies."[35] The rights of the fetus increase along a continuum, against the rights of the mother, so that there is no sharp line between *no* rights and *full* rights.

One might claim that Gillespie is guilty of the sorites paradox or the fallacy of "the argument from the beard." At issue is the precise number of hairs that makes one bald, or the exact number of pennies one may have and still be poor. No one knows. Gillespie's response is as follows. In dealing with continuums such an approach is not paradoxical. It is rather the only rational way to deal with the problem. "Given our awareness of the spectrum from poverty to riches, from baldness to a full head of hair, and from conception to adulthood, we can specify quite precisely where an individual falls along any of those spectrums. So precision is possible without drawing any lines; and in determining the rights of a being we can proceed in exactly the same fashion. Thus, when an adult requests an abortion, if it is seen as a conflict of rights case, the comparative strength of the rights of the being to be aborted is determined by its stage of development."[36]

In evaluating Gillespie's proposal it is only fair to concede that he is merely seeking a solution to the very specific line-drawing problem. Even though Gillespie may have devised an answer to the specific problem at hand, other objections to the approach may make it necessary to abandon the view. There are, however, good reasons for thinking that Gillespie's suggestion is seriously defective. First, his solution involves a redefinition of the key concepts of *person* and *rights*. Both now admit of degrees. Previously, the debate has been whether the terms

138

apply. Now they do apply but only partially. The question is whether it makes sense to talk of partial persons and partial rights. Gillespie responds: "So even if my use of 'person' and 'has rights' is revisionary, the facts of the situation require it, if those terms are to be adequate for discussing the morality of abortion."[37]

Second, Gillespie's proposal views the problem as one of conflicting rights. He does not mention, however, the possibility that there may be a hierarchy of rights. For instance, if the most fundamental right one has is the right to life, it would follow that the only conflict of rights that could result in abortion would be a case where the mother's right to life was threatened. If this be so, Gillespie's revision is not going to justify the kinds of abortions that the pro-abortionist wants.

Third, Gillespie's solution rests heavily on the belief that "we can specify *quite precisely* where an individual falls along any of those spectrums." This is clearly false. There would surely be continuous dispute about the exact position that any individual occupies on the spectrum. If Gillespie's assumption is false, as I believe, then his suggestion aggravates the problem rather than solving it. Previously, even if the line was drawn somewhat arbitrarily, one could decide whether the individual in question was a person with rights. Now, however, the situation is confused and less susceptible to resolution.

Finally, even if one can avoid these problems, the Gillespie proposal will be effective only against infanticide. Arguments can be made from it not only for abortion, but also for killing the severely retarded and the senile.

Such is the impasse between opponents and proponents of abortion over the status of the fetus. Is there any hope of resolving the difference of opinion? Not really. Roger Wertheimer puts it quite pessimistically when he says that the problem of the moral status of abortion is insoluble because the dispute centers on the fetus, and this is not a question of fact at all. Rather, it is a matter of how one responds to the facts.[38]

Do Nonexistent Persons Have Rights?

Given the seemingly insoluble difference on the status of the fetus, can any headway be made in the abortion debate? McLachlan argues that the ontological status of the fetus is not nearly as central a question as is generally thought. He suggests that the reason such a prominent place in abortion discussions is given to the fetus is attributable to two assumptions. First, only living, actual persons possess rights. Second, before one can have a duty, there must be someone who has a corresponding right.[39] McLachlan challenges both of these assumptions.

McLachlan tries to show through examples that nonexistent persons can have rights. The first example has to do with two friends. One tells the other a secret, whereupon the second promises never to reveal the secret. Suppose now that the teller of the secret dies. What happens to his right not to have his confidence betrayed? It survives, does it not? The second example relates a promise to place flowers on the grave of a friend. Does not the dead man have a right to expect this promise will be fulfilled? The third example is a bit different. Here the right does not arise out of contact or personal affinity. Although one has never met Wittgenstein, does he not have an obligation not to slander Wittgenstein? Or to put it in rights talk: Wittgenstein has a right not to be slandered. Thus, McLachlan concludes, "If I am correct in maintaining that a nonexistent person can have rights and that we can have duties towards him, then the question of the ontological status of the fetus need not be considered to be critically important and certainly not the central issue in the abortion debate."[40]

It seems that McLachlan has shown that nonexistent persons can have rights. But there is some question whether this will be of any significance to the abortion debate. The problem is this. In all of the examples cited the persons who had rights *had been* actual living persons and were *now* nonexistent persons. Further, it would appear that their rights were acquired while they were actual living people, and that these rights did not terminate with death. The issue is just the reverse in the abortion debate. Do nonexistent people or, more precisely, people who will someday come to be living persons have the same rights before birth that they will have after birth? It is just at this point that the determination rests so heavily on the status of the fetus.

The second point McLachlan addresses is the possibility that living persons have duties regarding abortion, where there is no actual existing person with a corresponding right. Again, McLachlan gives two examples to show that there may be duties where there are no actual existing persons or where there is no particular person possessing rights. First, if a man knew that through sexual union with his wife at a specific time a child would be conceived that would live in abject misery because of some physical ailment, he would have a duty to this nonexistent person to abstain. Second, in a somewhat different context, if someone had an abundance of food and those around him were starving, he would be obligated to give some food away, although no particular person among those who were starving could claim a right to the food.

Again, McLachlan is right and wrong. He seems to be right in claiming that one can owe a duty in spite of the fact that no existent or particular person possesses the corresponding right. But what he does not seem to see is that this is no help in determining what the duties are. To take the first example McLachlan uses, it seems that one's duty is not so much abstinence from sex if a miserable child will result as it is to see that a child that would suffer greatly should not be born. This could be accomplished by refraining from sex, or by indulging and seeking an abortion. And the status of the fetus will determine if only one or both of these alternatives is morally permissible.

Abortion and the Conflict of Rights

Before concluding this chapter, it is necessary to examine the abortion question from one final perspective. Is it possible to accept the anti-abortionists' claim that the fetus is a human person and still argue for a liberal view of abortion? Or to put it another way, can the question of the status of the fetus be transcended by demonstrating that even if the fetus is a human person, abortion can generally be justified? At least three arguments can be made from this perspective.

The first argument centers on the claim that a woman should have the right of control over her own body. Judith Thomson in a widely read article entitled "A Defense of Abortion" takes this position. She asks the reader to imagine himself waking up in bed with a famous violinist who is unconscious. The violinist has a fatal kidney ailment and only you have the right blood type to help. To unplug him would be to kill him. While you may not be happy with your new task, you are advised that it will only take nine months. The question you are faced with is this: Since all persons have a right to life, are you morally‑ obligated to spend the next nine months of your life keeping the violinist alive? Thomson's answer is no.[41]

Thomson then tries to draw a comparison to the situation facing a pregnant woman. Even assuming that the fetus is a human person and has a right to life, the mother's right to control of her own body outweighs the right of the child to live. Thomson claims that "the mother and the unborn child are not like two tenants in a small house which has, by an unfortunate mistake, been rented to both: the mother *owns* the house."[42] Thomson's point should not be missed. She is not denying the child's right to life. However, her claim is that the mother also has a right, and that right conflicts with the fetus.

A question is raised, however. Why should the mother's right always outweigh the child's? This rests on the distinction between what Thomson calls the minimally decent Samaritan and the good Samaritan. The good Samaritan goes out of his way, even at a cost to himself, to help one in need. On the other hand, the minimally decent Samaritan helps when it does not involve a cost to him, particularly a loss of his rights. Thomson concludes that all that is morally required is that one be a minimally decent Samaritan, and thus the fetus has no right to the mother's body unless she grants it. She says, "I am arguing only that the right to life does not guarantee having either a right to be given the use of or a right to be allowed continued use of another person's body—even if one needs it for life itself."[43]

Again, Thomson's discussion brings up many problems that need an answer. The first is the whole matter of the ownership of bodies. The idea is a bit curious. It is possible to sell a house that one owns, and in so doing give up ownership. But even a slave or prostitute can still call his body his own. Ownership of the fetus is less clear. If it is the property of the mother, should it not also be the property of the father? Or better yet, is not the body of the fetus the property of the fetus?

But there are much deeper issues connected with the matter of ownership. The major premise of this argument is that the woman has the right to do whatever she wants with her own body.[44] This is clearly false. A mother would perform a morally wrong action if she maimed herself so that she could not meet her obligation to care for her dependent children. Or would not a husband be failing in his duty toward his wife if he took drugs and became incapable of sexual relations?[45]

While Thomson has presented the argument for a woman's right to control her body in one of its most defensible forms, she has nonetheless failed to consider adequately the mother's responsibility for the fetus' presence in her body. The fetus has no choice in the matter. The mother's situation is quite different. While she may not have given explicit consent, most would agree that she has granted implicit consent to the use of her body by the embryo by engaging in intercourse. Admittedly, the view just articulated would allow for abortion in cases of rape, but this is far from abortion on demand. Furthermore, even in cases of rape, the mother may decide to bear the child.

The claim to ownership of one's body is at best a feeble argument for the right to kill. Mere ownership does not invest a person with the right to kill innocent people he finds trespassing on his property. On the contrary, one is likely to be held responsible if such persons are hurt on his property. This is particularly true given the special relation between a mother and her child. Atkinson says that "greater dependence produces greater, not less, responsibility. It is more wrong to maltreat one's child when he is two than when he is 15, precisely because the two-year-old is more dependent and thus more vulnerable to harm."[46]

Finally, Brody points out that Thomson fails to distinguish between two duties that one might have. There is the duty to save another's life. Here Thomson's distinction between the good Samaritan and the minimally decent Samaritan has applicability. One has a moral duty to help save a life only if it does not cost the rescuer his rights. For instance, one is not morally obligated to save a patient with a malfunctioning kidney if such help would result in the loss of the donor's life. Such an action is supererogatory. This, however, is quite different from one's duty not to take a person's life. It is this latter obligation that is violated when a mother aborts a child that does not threaten her life.[47]

A second variety of argument that might be used to justify abortions regardless of the personhood of the fetus is to claim that it is morally wrong to bring a child into the world who is unwanted and will thus suffer mental and physical privation.

As with the other arguments that we have examined, there are numerous difficulties with this one. This argument is convincing only if the principle that underlies it is sound. That principle is that an action is justified if it produces desirable consequences, in this case the destruction of an unwanted fetus. However, almost any action, no matter how immoral, can be justified by this criterion.

Moreover, the way in which the unwanted-child argument is presented hides the real source of the problem. The usual description makes it appear that there is some deficiency in the fetus and the fetus is responsible for it, when in fact the deficiency is in the parents. There are, to be sure, cases of reasonable hardship. Possibly the parents cannot care for the child because of health; perhaps the child is illegitimate. Such circumstances may justify putting up the child for adoption, but hardly do they excuse killing the embryo. On the other hand, if the real description of the situation is that the parents are heartless, selfish cowards, they would *not* be justified in killing those who are inconvenient to them.[48]

Moreover, it is extremely difficult to know whether an unwanted pregnancy will result in an unwanted child who will not be loved and will possibly be abused. As a matter of fact, given the large number of childless couples who desperately want to adopt, it is by no means true that the aborted embryos are unwanted.

Finally, the same argument could be used to justify killing infants, the insane, and the severely retarded. If a mother cannot afford an abortion, why should she not give birth at home and then kill the child?

Closely related to the unwanted-child argument is the claim that every child born into the world has the right to be loved. The implication seems to be that if a child will not be loved, then the mother is justified in seeking an abortion. Careful examination of this attempt to justify abortion shows that it too is faulty. If one would be better off with something than without it, it does not follow that he has a right to the thing. Clearly, every child would be better off with a $10,000 trust fund established at his birth, but does this mean that he has a *right* to such a fund? Analogously, a newborn child is better off loved, but does this constitute a right? If so, this is a heavy weight indeed to hang around the neck of the fetus, especially if the fetus can be killed because of it! Remember, too, the person who is making the determination is seldom disinterested.

Similar justification could be given in support of killing fussy infants, as well as retarded, elderly, and paraplegic persons.

The inescapable conclusion is that if rights and duties are cor-relative, the right of the fetus to be loved implies a correlative duty on the parents' part to love that child.

From the preceding discussion some deductions can be made:

1. With the exception of the privacy argument (the mother's control of her body) the abortion arguments on the side of the mother are essentially social in nature: population control, the sexual freedom of women, quality of life, and the reduction of ADC payments.

2. On the other hand, the arguments favoring the fetus are primarily individual-oriented, involving the interweaving of metaphysical and genetic considerations: the human potential-ity of, and the DNA or genetic structure of the embryo.

3. While it is difficult, and perhaps impossible, to convince a pro-abortionist of the personhood of the fetus, nevertheless from a purely ethical point of view it still makes sense to de-mand that human life should not be arbitrarily terminated, particularly when less drastic solutions exist. Such solutions should be sought on the side of both the fetus and the mother. Having once been conceived, the fetus has no choice but to grow, just as it had no choice in its conception or its blond hair or blue eyes. Hence, the fetus is without recourse and remedy. The same is not true of the mother, who has at least three alternatives other than abortion. She can exercise initial will power by abstinence, which is grossly out of fashion today. She has the option to use contraception to prevent the unwanted child. And finally, given the birth of the child, the mother can allow the living but unwanted infant to be put up for adoption. While this approach does not entirely resolve the confrontation between the two sides in the debate, it does make it clear that it is the fetus who is the innocent victim, and it is the mother who controls, at least in some human sense, the beginning of life and thus should take the necessary precautions to prevent the conception and subsequent destruction of it.

4. Finally, from the standpoint of ethics, it has been argued throughout that any reason that can be offered in support of abortion can in fact be used to justify infanticide, killing of the retarded and insane, and even involuntary euthanasia. It is impossible to draw a *moral* distinction between abortion and these other acts. Conversely, if a reason is unacceptable for infanticide, it is equally unacceptable for abortion. At the heart

of moral reasoning is the belief that equals should be treated equally. Inequality of treatment must be justified by some *morally relevant* difference. It is just such a difference that cannot be specified. If one is committed to the support of abortion, he must also be committed to involuntary euthanasia if he is to be consistent. It should be clear then that an attack on one form of human life represents an attack on other forms. The dignity and sanctity of life are too precious to be so easily eroded.

Notes

1. *Roe v. Wade* (1973).

2. R. B. Brandt, "The Morality of Abortion," *Monist,* 56 (1972), pp. 503–5.

3. There are some ethicists and theologians, particularly in the Roman Catholic Church, who would hold that abortion is *always* and *unconditionally* wrong, even if the life of the mother is threatened. It is their claim that abortion involves intervention and is thus killing. On the other hand, even should the mother and child both die, this is not a case of killing; rather, it involves letting them die. This position is not discussed because it seems so obviously wrong, but it is used by pro-abortionists to characterize anti-abortionists as heartless.

4. Germain Grisez, *Abortion: The Myths, the Realities, and the Arguments* (New York: Corpus Books, 1970), pp. 274ff.

5. *Roe v. Wade* (1973).

6. Gary M. Atkinson, "The Morality of Abortion," *International Philosophical Quarterly,* 14 (1974), pp. 356–57.

7. Grisez, *Myths,* p. 274. See also John T. Noonan, Jr., ed., *The Morality of Abortion: Legal and Historical Perspectives* (Cambridge, Mass.: Harvard University Press, 1970) and James M. Humber, "The Case against Abortion," *Thomist,* 39 (1975), pp. 65–66.

8. Grisez, *Myths,* pp. 274ff.

9. *Ibid.*

10. *Ibid.*

11. R. J. Gerber, "Abortion: Parameters for Decision," *Ethics,* 82 (1971), pp. 143–44. This same article appeared also in *International Philosophical Quarterly,* 11 (1971).

12. Daniel Callahan, *Abortion: Law, Choice, and Morality* (New York: Macmillan, 1970), p. 397.

13. Paul Ramsey, "Abortion: A Review Article," *Thomist,* 37 (1973), pp. 188–89.

14. Joseph T. Mangan, S.J., "The Wonder of Myself: Ethical-Theological Aspects of Direct Abortion," *Theological Studies,* 31 (1970), pp. 132–33.

15. *Ibid.*

16. Grisez, *Myths,* p. 26.

17. Ramsey, "Review Article," p. 193. See also Paul Ramsey, "The Morality of Abortion," in Daniel H. Labby, ed., *Life or Death: Ethics and Options* (Seattle: University of Washington Press, 1968), p. 63 n., for a similar position.

18. Humber, "Case against Abortion," p. 68.

19. H. Tristram Engelhardt, Jr., "The Ontology of Abortion," *Ethics,* 84 (1973), p. 219. See also Ludwig Wittgenstein, *Philosophical Investigations,* trans. G. E. M. Anscombe (Oxford: Basil Blackwell, 1963), p. 116.

20. Engelhardt, p. 219. See also Wittgenstein, *Investigations,* p. 116.

21. Humber, "Case against Abortion," pp. 65–66.

22. R. M. Hare, "Abortion and the Golden Rule," *Philosophy and Public Affairs,* 4 (1975), p. 206.

23. *Ibid.,* p. 207.

24. *Ibid.,* p. 208.

25. *Ibid.,* p. 209.

26. *Ibid.*

27. Engelhardt, "Ontology of Abortion," pp. 223–25.

28. Atkinson, "Morality of Abortion," p. 351.

29. Mary Anne Warren, "On the Moral and Legal Status of Abortion," *Monist,* 57 (1973), p. 59.

30. R. Werner, "Hare on Abortion," *Analysis,* 36 (1976), p. 178.

31. Warren, "Moral and Legal Status," pp. 47–48; 52ff.

32. Ramsey, "Review Article," pp. 184–85.

33. Atkinson, "Morality of Abortion," p. 350.

34. *Ibid.*, p. 352.

35. Norman C. Gillespie, "Abortion and Human Rights," *Ethics*, 87 (1976), p. 238.

36. *Ibid.*, p. 239.

37. *Ibid.*, pp. 242–43.

38. Roger Wertheimer, "Understanding the Abortion Argument," *Philosophy and Public Affairs*, 1 (1971), pp. 67–95.

39. Hugh V. McLachlan, "Must We Accept Either the Conservative or Liberal View on Abortion?" *Analysis*, 37 (1977), p. 198.

40. *Ibid.*, p. 200.

41. Judith Jarvis Thomson, "A Defense of Abortion," *Philosophy and Public* Affairs, 1 (1971), pp. 47–66.

42. *Ibid.*, p. 53.

43. *Ibid.*, p. 56.

44. One might argue that the proposed answer begs the question since it assumes a conflict of rights, i. e., the right of the mother to control her body and that of the child to life. Yet the point at issue is not whether the fetus has rights, but whether the major premise of the "privacy argument" is true.

45. Atkinson, "Morality of Abortion," p. 353.

46. *Ibid.*

47. Baruch Brody, "Thomson on Abortion," *Philosophy and Public Affairs*, 1 (1972), pp. 335–40.

48. Atkinson, "Morality of Abortion," p. 355.

7   Abortion and Women's Lib
Susan T. Foh

The right to abortion is not a peripheral or secondary idea in feminist ideology. It is central and basic; it has top priority. To abolish all laws restricting abortions is to get to the root of the problem for women. The feminist argument for abortion is phrased as the right of a woman to control her own body or her own reproduction. This right is seen as the foundation for all of the woman's other rights.

The first feminist movement in the 19th century avoided all sexual issues and focused on social and economic issues. The 19th-century feminists were anxious to reassure society that they did not want to disrupt it by challenging marriage and family. Their demands finally dwindled down to one—the right to vote; and when this goal was reached in 1920, the women's movement lost its force. Even at the beginning of the current feminist movement, the area of sexual rights was hardly discussed and the abortion issue was avoided. *The Feminine Mystique* (1963) by Betty Friedan, the book that raised women's consciousnesses and, in a sense, began the movement, did not develop the idea of the woman's right to control her own body.

> Even to [Friedan's] probing mind, sex was still ostracized from the grand pattern of feminine emancipation. "I was so obsessed with the issue of equality that I couldn't face the meaning of sex," she explained. Another neofeminist leader, Ms. Jean Faust, concluded, "We were all blocked at first by traditional labels. We were afraid of being called 'loose women' if we included abortion in our platform."[1]

But by 1967, a year after the founding of NOW (the National Organization for Women), Friedan and the young leadership succeeded in getting an abortion plank into their program. Lawrence Lader, a crusader in the fields of birth control and population control, affirms the necessity of this move:

> Friedan and neofeminism erupted on a wave of technology. For it was the technology of contraception, the birth control pill, that made possible the radicalization of women. Only when technology—and abortion is a crucial step in this process—allowed women to free themselves from the prison of incessant childbearing could they grapple with the possibility of achieving themselves on every plane. By bringing NOW, and eventually women's lib into the abortion campaign, Friedan ensured that the struggle for feminine liberation was solidly rooted in the one base that could turn theory into reality—a woman's control over her own body and procreation.[2]

All other rights—social, economic, political—depend on the fundamental right of the woman to control her own body.

> Without the full capacity to limit her own reproduction, a woman's other "freedoms" are tantalizing mockeries that cannot be exercised. With it, the others cannot long be denied, since the chief rationale for denial disappears.[3]

How does the control of her own body lead to other rights or freedoms? It does so symbolically and actually. On a symbolic level:

> Because women have wombs and bear children, and because technical control of the reproductive function has always been imperfect—as it still is today—society has ultimately always defined woman as a childbearer—that is, as she relates to children and to men, rather than as an individual.
> . . . different reproductive roles are *the* basic dichotomy in humankind, and have been used to ratio-

nalize all the other, ascribed differences between men and women and to justify all the oppression women have suffered.[4]

Woman has come to be defined and identified by one of her roles or functions, motherhood, to the exclusion of others; motherhood becomes her sole definition because it is inevitable and obvious and belongs only to her. Motherhood becomes a symbol for all women—single or married, pregnant or not, young or old; as mothers, women as a whole are considered already occupied with children and therefore not able or suited for work. They are to be protected.

Because women bear children, they are assigned as their primary responsibility the care of children and the home. Because women have been socialized into this role and because someone must take care of children, women are actually prevented from full participation in business, politics, education, and so on. Their time is taken up with washing dishes and changing diapers. As mothers, they are also economically dependent on someone else (usually their husbands) for support. As for those women who work outside the home, the majority have *jobs,* not careers or professions, because the possibility of pregnancy and the consequent interruption of their work mean that they are job risks for employers.

> So long as sexual pleasure could not be enjoyed without the anxiety of a possible pregnancy, women seeking wider and more demanding participation in professions or politics really had an either-or choice of marriage *or* a career, while those who attempted the combination did so with a sense of anxiety that can be anathema to creativity in work.[5]

With the control of her reproduction in hand, the woman is able to escape the possibility of pregnancy. She can pursue a career without dread of interruption and achieve economic independence. The control of her own reproduction enables the woman to dethrone the feminine mystique (a woman's fulfillment lies in children and home) in her own mind, in action, and in the minds of others. When she is no longer confined by motherhood, she shatters the symbol of motherhood.

Friedan is explicit: a woman's right to control her own body means the abolition of laws prohibiting abortion. The decision whether or not to bear a child belongs to the one most intimately involved—the woman, according to the feminists.

> [NOW] said that it is the inalienable human right of every woman to control her own reproductive process. To establish that right would require that all laws penalizing abortion be repealed, removed from the penal code; the state would not be empowered either to force or prevent a woman from having an abortion.[6]

The woman's right to control her own reproduction is the main feminist argument for abortion on demand.

> Proposals for "reform" [of abortion laws] are based on the notion that abortions must be regulated, meted out to deserving women under an elaborate set of rules designed to provide "safeguards against abuse." At least the old laws require only the simple, if vague, test of danger to life, whereas the new bills make it quite clear that a woman's own decision is meaningless without the "right" reasons, the concurrence of her family, and the approval of a bunch of strange medical men. Repeal is based on the quaint idea of *justice:* that abortion is a woman's right and that no one can veto her decision and compel her to bear a child against her will. All the excellent supporting reasons—improved health, lower birth and death rates, freer medical practice, the separation of church and state, happier families, sexual privacy, lower welfare expenditures—are only embroidery on the basic fabric: *woman's right to limit her own reproduction.*
>
> It is *this* rationale that the new woman's movement has done so much to bring to the fore.[7]

In choosing to frame their argument for the right to abortion on demand as the right to control one's own body, the feminists made a politic decision on two accounts.

1. They shift the emphasis away from the unborn child to the mother. Though the fetus is not completely forgotten, his sig-

nificance and reality are minimized. Philosopher Donald DeMarco gives a sample of how this is done by antilocution (speaking against someone):

> Philosopher Joseph Fletcher [an Episcopal priest who favors abortion] states, "There is no such thing as an unborn baby." According to Fletcher the fetus is mere "gametic material." Pro-abortion evangelist William Baird describes the early fetus as "marmalade." Author Philip Wylie calls the fetus "protoplasmic rubbish, a gobbet of meat." A political leader announces over the radio that "at 20 weeks' pregnancy you cannot tell the developing fetus from a cancer or a mass of flesh." At a legislative hearing on abortion, university students and faculty members testify that the "fetus is not human. It is a mass of tissue." Women's Liberation representatives argue that the fetus is part of the woman's body.[8]

Regardless of whether or not the fetus is viewed as a person to be protected by the Constitution, the fetus is definitely not marmalade, rubbish, a gobbet of meat, or part of the woman's body. That the fetus is part of his mother's body has no physiological justification. He has his own unique genetic code, a combination of his mother's and father's genes. He has a separate nervous system and circulation system and his own skeleton, musculature, brain, heart, and other vital organs. The fact that the fetus is not part of the woman's body undermines the feminists' argument; the right to control one's own body does not justify abortion because the fetus is not part of the woman's body. The fetus is deliberately misrepresented in order to justify his extermination.

> It is much easier to think of killing "the product of conception" rather than destroying an embryo. It would also be easier to kill a fetus than to kill an unborn baby.[9]

Semantics plays an important part in the feminist campaign for abortion.

2. Feminists emphasize the mother's *rights* in a country where the individual's rights and liberties are treasured and

154

carefully guarded. It is hard for Americans to oppose anything that is presented to us as an individual's right or freedom. Feminists fan the flame by contrasting the *right* of the woman to control her own reproduction by means of contraception *and* abortion with *interference* by the state. Notice the persuasive rhetoric.

> It seemed to me [Lader] that for the state to force any woman to bear a child against her will was a flagrant and brutal abuse of personal liberty.[10]

Friedan passionately argues for the woman's right:

> What right has any man to say to any woman, "You must bear this child"? What right has the state to say it? The child-bearing decision is a woman's right and not a technical question needing the sanction of the state, nor should the state control access to birth control devices.
>
> This question can only really be confronted in terms of the basic personhood and dignity of woman, which is violated forever if she does not have the right to control her own reproductive process. And the heart of this idea goes far beyond abortion and birth control.[11]

Feminists particularly do not want men telling them what to do with their bodies, and the state is run by men. Women are the ones who get pregnant, they protest; men just make laws regulating that pregnancy.

To accentuate women's rights, the feminists picture laws restricting abortion as assaults on the personhood of women; this approach obscures the question of the status and rights of the fetus. According to feminist logic, the choice is between being for abortion on demand or being against women. By couching the abortion issue in terms of the woman's rights, the pro-abortionists aim to appeal to a "higher" morality (higher than the morality that protects the life of the fetus).

> What we were seeking, after all, seemed so profoundly just and humane. It was simply the right of personal decision, the right of a woman to control

155

the creative powers of her body, to bring into the world only a child she truly wanted and loved.[12]

Someone had insisted, like an abolitionist hiding an escaped slave in 1850, that no matter how the law read, there was a higher law of moral decency that demanded no woman should be forced into an unwanted pregnancy, or the alternative horror of underworld abortion.[13]

The main problem with the feminist argument for abortion, the right of the woman to control her own body or her own reproduction, is that it is based on a misrepresentation. It is based on the notion that the fetus is a part of the woman's body and therefore under her absolute control. The fetus is not part of the woman's body, and therefore his separate (though dependent) existence and the implications of that separate existence should be taken into account. The feminists cannot proclaim women's rights, liberties, and freedoms as an adequate and convincing argument for the abolition of prohibitive abortion laws. The feminists argue that the woman's rights have priority over those of the fetus, but they fail to weigh the rights to liberty and pursuit of happiness (what are at stake for the woman) against the right to life (what is at stake for the fetus).

What does the right to control one's own body mean? The feminists do not discuss this question in any detail.

Margaret Sanger was perhaps the first American champion of the woman's right to control her own body. She wrote:

Woman herself has wrought that bondage through her reproductive powers and while enslaving herself has enslaved the world. Hers, too, is the love life that dies first under the blight of too prolific breeding. Within her is wrapped up the future of the race—it is hers to make or mar. All of these considerations point unmistakably to one fact—it is woman's duty as well as her privilege to lay hold of the means of freedom. Whatever men may do, she cannot escape the responsibility. . . .

The basic freedom of the world is woman's freedom. A free race cannot be born of slave mothers. . . . No woman can call herself free until she can choose consciously whether she will or will not be a mother.[14]

For Sanger, the right to control one's own reproduction meant contraception but not abortion. She opposed abortion all of her life. Lader evaluates her attitude: ". . . she was right in the context of her time. But the context had changed by 1962."[15] For Lader, the changed context is a matter of medical advances and increased volume: 550,000 unwanted births each year and 1,000,000 secret abortions, according to his statistics. It would seem that technology and statistics would extend the woman's right to control her own reproduction to include abortion as well as contraception. Lader uses a utilitarian argument, not a philosophical or moral argument, to justify a woman's right to control her own body. The nature of the fetus is not considered. The abortionist ethic is pragmatic; the morality of abortion, the destruction of a human fetus, is not really the issue for the abortionist.

At this point, it is appropriate to make a distinction between contraception and abortion—a distinction that the feminists are loath to make.

> . . . whether something "is" contraception or abortion is actually of little consequence in evaluating the result: the goal is the prevention of an unwanted birth, and whatever will achieve this aim safely and surely we can simply call "birth control" and be done with it.[16]

This feminist assumes that the end justifies the means—a questionable moral imperative.

Contraception prevents impregnation. Egg and sperm, each possessing one half of the chromosomes for a human being, are prevented from uniting; neither egg nor sperm alone has any capacity for reproduction. Abortion may be natural (commonly termed miscarriage) or induced. We are concerned here only with artificially induced abortions. An induced abortion destroys or kills the fetus. The difference between contraception and abortion is that another party is involved. When the egg and sperm unite, a human organism, to say the least, with its own unique genetic code, is formed. The miracle of life begins

—a trite but true statement. The life of the zygote is a life separate from that of the mother; and without interference, the zygote will normally become an adult human being. There is continuity between the zygote and the newborn child and the adult. Contraception intends to eliminate the possibility of impregnation; at the very least, it must be said that abortion destroys a potential human being, a living human organism that will develop into what everyone recognizes as a human being. Consequently, the justification for abortion is not the same as for contraception.

When Sanger argued for the woman's right to decide through contraception when and whether to become a mother, she spoke in terms of accepting responsibility, of duty. Men do not concern themselves with birth control, she said, nor are they most intimately involved in the birth and rearing of children. Women must, therefore, take the responsibility for birth control (that is, contraception). In contrast, the abortionists of today allow for irresponsibility; they include, in their mention of contraceptive failure, the fact that contraception is often not used.

> But since many contraceptives had an inherent rate of error, or could fail, or were prescribed erroneously, or *simply not used in a moment of abandon,* contraception without the supporting right of abortion condemned women to biological chance.[17] (Emphasis mine)

> Despite the gains of the birth control movement, most contraceptives still had a broad margin of error or misuse, or *were not used at all.*[18] (Emphasis mine)

> It is one of the psychological weaknesses of contraception that it requires the rational anticipation of an abrogation of reason—which affronts both the logician and the poet in us.[19]

Sanger wanted women to take the responsibility foisted upon them. The current abortion movement wants to legalize abortion to relieve women of any responsibility for their actions (acknowledging that intercourse may produce a pregnancy) or inaction (failure to use contraception). The fact is that if contraception were practiced responsibly and consistently, the number of "problem" or "unwanted" pregnancies and the requests or desires for abortions would decrease remarkably. The failure rate of the pill is approximately 1 percent, or one failure per 100 woman-years of use, and the failure rate for the diaphragm is 2 percent.

Many of the contraceptive failures reported result from inconsistent usage of contraceptive devices. The woman who desperately does not want to have a child should use a contraceptive device according to the directions, even if it offends the poet in her. For the woman who would consider abortion the answer to pregnancy, the avoidance of pregnancy through contraception should outweigh the inconvenience of the necessary forethought and even the reduction of pleasure. For extra insurance, the woman can avoid intercourse during her fertile time of the month. The woman who is sure she does not want children or any more children can be sterilized. Abortion is not the only answer.

The preceding point, to avoid pregnancy through contraception, raises a pertinent question: When does the woman's right to control her own body begin and end? It is an obvious suggestion that the right to control one's own body begins considerably before the need for abortion arises. The use of contraception requires the control of one's own body, self-control. But that sort of control is not what the feminists mean. If it were, there would be no clamor for the right to abortion. The epitome of self-control would provide the only foolproof method of contraception—abstinence.

Sexual intercourse involves a relinquishing of one's right to one's own body (for both man and woman). This should be self-evident from the nature of the act.

> Willingness to engage in physical intercourse includes the mutual promise of troth to bear the responsibility of the act. By that criterion most abortions are simply ruled out as immoral. Pregnancies resulting from affairs are not exceptions since affairs are voluntary matters. At the same time, the mutual-troth character of intercourse destroys the argument that the woman has control of her own body and that therefore abortion is her sole concern. Of course a woman as an individual controls her own

159

body. The point is that both the man and the woman voluntarily give up their bodies to their mates when they have sexual intercourse. The resulting pregnancy is their mutual responsibility.[20]

Because the woman voluntarily participates in intercourse, she gives up the right to absolute sovereignty over her body. If she becomes pregnant, she has already given the father a right to and responsibility for the unborn child. Mother and father share the responsibility for the child.

Feminists attempt to eliminate this responsibility by legalizing abortion. But sexual intercourse carries responsibility because it always involves the possibility of pregnancy. That possibility is part of the reason traditional morality and Christianity teach that sex should take place only within marriage, a stable relation between a man and a woman in which a child can be cared for.

One pro-abortionist, Dr. Garrett Hardin, dismisses the father's right to a say in the fate of his unborn child. According to Dr. Hardin, the woman need only tell her husband (or, I suppose, the man who thinks it is his child) that the child is not his. Dr. Hardin does not discuss the morality (i.e., is it a true statement) of such a tactic and he does not deal with how the woman would know beforehand which man was the father. If more than one man was involved, she could not be sure. To lie about the unborn child's paternity or to conceal his paternity from the father in order to prevent the father from opposing an abortion would be a power play on the woman's part—a tactic women have castigated men for using against women. Dr. Hardin then asks:

> Or, in terms of public policy, do we want to pass laws which give men the right to compel their wives to be pregnant? Psychologically, such compulsion is akin to rape. Is it in the public interest to encourage rape?[21]

Dr. Hardin's notion of compulsory pregnancy is a clever reversal of reality. Husbands do not force their wives to bear children. In a sense, it is "nature" that compels the woman to be pregnant after the egg is fertilized. Before the egg is fertilized, it is a matter of mutual consent; that is, a man and a woman

160

"get the woman pregnant." The woman is responsible for her condition (except in cases of actual rape). And it is surely a misnomer to call protecting a life, preventing someone from destroying a life, "rape." The woman's right to the sovereign control of her own body ends when she consents to intercourse. In sexual intercourse, she gives a man some control of her body and vice versa; and they both have rights to and responsibilities for the fruit of that act, the child, before and after birth.

Ironically, the feminists, who wish to deny the father of the unborn child the right to oppose that child's abortion, advocate that fathers take a more active part in raising children. The feminist ideal is child care shared equally by men and women. But if the father is formally and legally denied rights to his unborn children, it seems unlikely that fathers or men in general will be encouraged to take a more active role in child care.

There is another note of irony in the feminists' cry for abortion on demand as part of the woman's right to control her own body. The feminists oppose the concept of woman as a sex object. Yet with freedom from unwanted pregnancy after the fact, which abortion guarantees, women are made more susceptible to exploitation as sex objects. Feminists have been the most vocal supporters of abortion on demand; nevertheless, a survey taken by Judith Blake, a demographer, reveals that the non-Catholic, male, well-educated establishment is the group that supports abortion most strongly (numerically). Feminists should ask why the "sexist" regime supports abortion. The reason may be that abortion gives them more sexual freedom without worry about paternity.[22]

The woman's right to control her own body, which the feminists claim as an inalienable right, cannot be conceived of as absolute. For instance, it does not give her the right to kill herself; suicide is illegal. It does not give her the freedom to do whatever she wants at the expense of other people. Traffic rules are an example. They limit our freedom to drive as we wish, yet ultimately they preserve our freedom because they protect our lives. We are inextricably bound to one another; what we do affects other people. No woman is an island. Everyone cannot have unlimited freedom. The woman's right to control her own body, a simple phrase and a seemingly reasonable demand, is more complicated and has greater implications than may be apparent at first.

In traffic laws, the state has the right to limit the individual's freedom to protect that individual and others. In the cases of "problem" pregnancies, the state also has the right to limit the mother's freedom in order to protect the life of another, the fetus, to guard the father's right to his child, and even to protect the mother's health. There is some evidence indicating that legalized abortion affects the health of the mother adversely in the long run. In another chapter, the psychological effects of abortion on the mother have been discussed. In countries where abortion is legal, statistics show the adverse physical effects of abortion on women. A 1969 survey of the office of the prime minister in Japan reported these complications resulting from induced abortions: 9 percent sterility after three years; 14 percent habitual spontaneous abortion; 4 percent extrauterine pregnancies; 17 percent menstrual irregularities; 20 percent abdominal pains; 19 percent dizziness; 27 percent headaches; 3 percent frigidity; 13 percent exhaustion; and 3 percent neurosis.[23] Dr. Alfred Kotasek of Czechoslovakia writes:

> Furthermore, as noticed recently, a high incidence of cervical incompetence results from interruption of pregnancy that raises the number of spontaneous abortions to 30–40 percent. These legal abortions affect subsequent pregnancies and births. We rather often observe complications such as rigidity of the os, placenta adherens, placenta accreta, and atony of the uterus.[24]

The phrase, "a woman's right to control her own body," exhibits another problem, a problem psychologists, philosophers, and poets have observed in our society: alienation from self.

> As one pages through the limitless literature on abortion, he finds time and again, citations from women which identify their liberation with an escape from the tyranny of their bodies. One characteristic citation, from a woman who had just undergone an abortion, reads: "I just could not allow myself to feel so much at the mercy of my biology. I was damned if I was going to let my body dictate the rest of my life."[25]

The feminist demand suggests that the body is not an integral and genuine part of the woman; it is treated as if it were a piece of property she possessed, which she would either control or be controlled by. Her self (will or mind) is controller of the object (her body). This dualism denies that we are our bodies. Body does not exhaust the meaning of being a human being, but body is an essential part of being human.

In their campaign for abortion the feminists employ several secondary supporting arguments. These arguments are invalid primarily because they do not consider the status of the unborn child.

The pro-abortionists[26] claim that the reasons for restrictive abortion laws no longer exist, and therefore they should be abolished. They state that abortion laws were instituted in the 19th century in order to protect women from medical hazards and to stimulate the population. Today, the argument runs, advances in abortion technology have made it a safe operation, and overpopulation is a world problem. Consequently, the need for abortion laws has ended. However, before the abortion "reform" movement and before 1920, seven states forbade abortion simply because the rights of the unborn child must be protected.[27] The abortionist argument based on the origin of abortion laws can be defeated on its own terms. In addition, this argument depends only on a sort of legal precedent, which is not infallible.

Another approach used by pro-abortionists is to point to the legal difficulty in regulating abortions. Some state laws, formed on the American Law Institute model, allow abortion in cases of rape, incest, and probability of deformity; some take the mental health of the mother into account. But how can such laws be enforced? It is difficult to *prove* rape; and if the woman is married and has been having sexual relations with her husband, how can she know whose child she is carrying? How probable must deformity be before abortion is permitted? Does the expectant mother have to attempt suicide before her mental health is considered in jeopardy? The abortionists' answer is: Because abortion is more complex than murder (the mother's rights complicate it) and because laws that have tried to reflect this complexity have in practice been discriminatory and unable to reduce illegal abortions, abortion should not be a matter of law; it should be left to the individual conscience of the woman involved.[28] However, what is right or wrong and what is legal or illegal are not decided by what is easiest to enforce. Facility in law enforcement is desirable, but it is not the primary standard by which laws should be made.

Feminists complain that "reformed" abortion laws (such as the ALI model) institutionalize the unspoken definition of women as creatures too feeble-minded to decide for themselves whether or not they should have an abortion.[29] This reaction to the ALI model demonstrates the feminists' defensiveness. Laws, in general, do not insult the intelligence of the public, and the reformed abortion laws do not disparage the abilities of women. Laws are necessary not because individuals are unable to make decisions but because individuals tend to act in their own interest without sufficient regard for the welfare of others.

Pro-abortionists often cite statistics "proving" that laws that restrict abortions in practice discriminate against the poor. The rich can afford to leave the state or the country to obtain an abortion; they have the resources to find qualified doctors who will perform abortions. The poor do not have such options. The rights of the poor are to be protected; but if abortion is wrong—immoral—steps should be taken to apply the law to the rich as well as the poor. When the rich evade the law, any law, the route to go is not to relax the law so that both rich and poor can commit crimes. The measure to take is to enforce the law for the rich as well.

Abortion advocates also describe the horrors of underworld abortions and self-abortions. One feminist protests, "And we never even consider the ten thousand innocent women annually murdered by men who refuse to legalize abortion."[30] As in the case of discrimination against the poor, the step to take is to tighten the law rather than relax it. Underworld abortionists should be prosecuted. Rather than setting up free tax-supported abortion clinics, part of the answer is to establish more and better clinics to provide contraception and counseling. If she cannot adjust to having another child, the woman should be encouraged to give him up for adoption.

> The Catholic hierarchy and other religious dogmatists claimed they were protecting the rights of the fetus even if hundreds of thousands of unwanted children ended up in adoption services and foster homes, or became the victims of the "battered child" syndrome.[31]

164

In order to protect children from being unwanted and from physical abuse, we should destroy them as fetuses, say the pro-abortionists. This argument does not hold up.

> The turbulent future of an unwanted child can be avoided by aborting him. By extension, all possible death and disability can be eradicated by discontinuing the human race.[32]

Advocates of abortion claim to be concerned for the "spirit" of the child, which would be damaged if he felt unwanted, but can this concern be genuine if they would destroy the *life* of the child because it would inconvenience the mother? The pro-abortion slogan, "Every child should be wanted and needed," is appealing, and no one would want to disagree. However, the slogan is based on two erroneous assumptions: (1) women either want or do not want children, without ambivalence and without inconsistency; and (2) the reasons women want and need children are always legitimate.

The criterion of "unwantedness" can be challenged on other grounds.

> With the right-to-privacy ruling, the human fetus's right to life is judged to be conferred upon him by his mother. By being unwanted by his mother, the human fetus loses all claim to his existence. What could be a clearer case of arbitrary authoritarianism? The human fetus is nothing until the mother sanctions his existence by wanting or needing him. The human fetus is good only because he is wanted; he is not wanted because he is good. The wish of the mother outweighs the substance of the fetus. The fetus has no intrinsic value, goodness, or dignity. The mother, in conferring value upon him through mere approval, becomes a symbol of power rather than love.[33]

The argument based on the unwantedness of the fetus fails to account for the objective reality of the fetus and his intrinsic value.

The child-abuse argument is not borne out by the facts. Dr. Edward Lenoski of the University of Southern California stud-

165

ied 400 cases of battered children over a four-and-a-half-year period. Ninety percent of the women he surveyed had planned the pregnancy that resulted in the abused child.[34] Mary Van Stolk in *The Battered Child in Canada,* chapter 4, states that the "dominant cohesive factor" in the personality of the child batterer is his "lack of identification with the child as a human being."[35] The premise that the fetus is not a human being can lead to doubts about the humanity of the child and so contributes to child abuse.

Overpopulation is another so-called reason for supporting abortion on demand. Overpopulation is a problem, but it is not one that justifies genocide or infanticide, although both means have been used in the past. The taking of human life is not justified by the problem. There are other solutions to the problems of overpopulation: conservation of natural resources, development of new sources of energy, farming the ocean, contraception, voluntary sterilization, and even the development of the moon. Overpopulation cannot be used as an excuse for abortion because it does not consider the status of the fetus.

Is abortion right or wrong? To ask such a question implies the existence of an absolute standard of morality, which pro-abortionists generally ignore. Dr. Hardin sidesteps the question of the morality of abortion:

> People who worry about the moral danger of abortion do so because they think of the fetus as a human being, hence equate feticide with murder. Whether the fetus is or is not a human being is a matter of definition, not fact; and we can define any way we wish. In terms of the human problem involved [the rights of the woman], it would be unwise to define the fetus as human (hence tactically unwise ever to refer to the fetus as an "unborn child").[36]

Objective reality is denied; the nature of the fetus is made to seem as if it depends on our opinion of it. We cannot define any way we wish, if words are to have any meaning or validity. Words and meaning should correspond as closely as possible to objective reality. Either abortion is moral or abortion is immoral (the situation in which the mother's *life* is in danger being the only exceptional case, because the choice is between two human lives). How we define the terms of the question will clarify the issue insofar as they correspond to reality or muddle it insofar as they do not. Expediency, such as Dr. Hardin suggests (if the fetus is not considered a human being, there are no conflicting rights; the expectant mother simply gets her wishes), justified by complete subjectivity ("we can define any way we wish"), is an irresponsible and arbitrary choice of standards. To state the problem clearly does not necessarily make the answer simple and easy, as Dr. Hardin assumes; Dr. Hardin begins with a simple solution and then states the issue in terms that correspond with his preconceived answer. Dr. Hardin neglects two indisputable facts: the fetus is human genetically, and the fetus is alive. He is a human life.

Supporters of abortion argue that the state should not enforce morality. This objection raises the question: If the law does not enforce morality, what does it enforce? Surely, there is some concurrence between the areas covered by morality and by law, such as murder and theft. There is also a divergence; for instance, there is no law against lying (although there are laws implying that lying is undesirable, such as laws against perjury and laws enforcing legal contracts). Does abortion fall into the category of moral law that should be enforced by the state? Earlier, we have answered yes, on the ground that the rights of more than one person must be taken into account, those of the fetus and those of the father. In addition, the physical well-being of a human life (the fetus) is at stake.

In conjunction with their complaint that morality should not be enforced by law, the pro-abortionists disparage groups that oppose liberalized abortion on moral grounds, especially religious groups. They decry the "dictatorship over these rights [of a woman to use her body as she sees fit] by puritan moralists and religious dogmatists."[37] Abortion laws "became mainly a bludgeon against women, an enforcement device to support moral and religious codes."[38]

> The puritan tradition linked sex with evil and guilt. To the puritan mind, laws against contraception and abortion were intended to punish and degrade women, and above all, to deprive them of the possibility of enjoying sex for its own sake.[39]

The propriety of any concurrence between morality and law is denied. And the motivation of Christian groups is misrepresented (as is the puritan concept of sex); the motive behind opposition to abortion on demand is not to degrade or punish women but to protect the life of the fetus. Even when the true motive is recognized, it is sometimes ridiculed:

> The feminist coalition struck back, "I deplore the arrogance and presumption of the Catholic Church in this matter," one feminist told a Seattle meeting. "You believe the fetus is a human being. Some people still believe witches ride around on broomsticks and a lot of other medieval, mystic hangovers."[40]

Ridicule is an easier weapon to use than reason.

A fairer description of the motivation of the Christian (or "puritan moralist" or "religious dogmatist") is:

> When the Christian defends the fetus's right to life, he is no more imposing a value than he would be in deterring a person from suicide or giving someone artificial respiration. Values may be said to be imposed only when they do not correspond to an essential human need.[41]

Feminists regard laws restricting abortion as an example of misogyny, the hatred of women. Women are seen as innocent victims of illegal abortions and of the cruel punishment of being forced to carry a baby to term if they become pregnant. Ms. Lana Phelan claims, "Abortion laws are a lie, a farce, and slavery, in its cruellest sense."[42] The right to abortion should be granted to women because society has been stacked against women.[43] Semantics and rhetoric play an important part in defending this feminist idea. (Consider: can pregnancy really be defined as slavery, since the condition was caused by a voluntary action on the part of the woman?)

> Those who caution us to play down the woman's rights argument are only trying to put off the inevitable day when the society must face and eradicate the misogynistic roots of the present situation. And anyone who has spoken publicly about abortion from

the feminist point of view knows all too well that it is *feminism*—not abortion—that is the really disturbing idea.[44]

Ms. Cisler has a point when she says feminism is the issue. To oppose abortion may turn out to be to oppose feminism (because abortion is necessary in the attempt to eliminate the basic difference between men and women); however, to oppose abortion is not equivalent to misogyny.

Abortion and feminism are closely related. The right to abortion is a necessary and foundational part of the feminists' vision; and their justification for abortion, the woman's right to control her own body, has implications far beyond abortion, as Friedan announces (quoted earlier). The goal of women's liberation is complete equality between the sexes. One feminist carries this goal as far as it can go:

> . . . I happen to think that science must be used to either release women from biological reproduction— or to allow men to experience the process also.[45]

One opponent of women's lib observes the connection between the goals of feminism and abortion.

> . . . of all the injustices perpetrated upon women through the centuries, the most oppressive is the cruel fact that women have babies and men do not. Within the confines of the women's liberationist ideology, therefore, the abolition of this overriding inequality of women becomes the primary goal. This goal must be achieved at any and all costs—to the woman herself, to the baby, to the family, and to society. Women must be made equal to men in their ability *not* to become pregnant and *not* to be expected to care for babies they may bring into the world.
>
> This is why women's liberationists are compulsively involved in the drive to make abortion and child-care centers for all women, regardless of religion or income, both socially acceptable and government-financed.[46]

Friedan states:

> The changes necessary to bring about that equality were, and still are, very revolutionary indeed. They involve a sex-role revolution for men and women which will restructure all our institutions: child rearing, education, marriage, the family, the architecture of the home, the practice of medicine, work, politics, the economy, religion, psychological theory, human sexuality, and the very evolution of the race.[47]

Abortion is only one part, but a basic part, of a complete revolution. What are the implications of feminist ideology?

One consequence of the right to abortion is its contribution to the sexual revolution, a cherished feminist goal. The primary reason for this goal is perhaps the destruction of patriarchy, families in which a man is head, and the double standard. Kate Millett says:

> A sexual revolution would require, perhaps first of all, an end of traditional sexual inhibitions and taboos, particularly those that threaten patriarchal monogamous marriage: homosexuality, "illegitimacy," adolescent, pre- and extra-marital sexuality. . . . The goal of the revolution would be a permissive single standard of sexual freedom . . .[48]

Lader recognizes the link between abortion and the sexual revolution:

> To advocate the right of abortion meant tearing down the key bulwark against immorality. Whether for the single girl or married woman, it meant destroying the ultimate punishment of sex, and allowing the pleasure of sex for its own sake without the concomitant obligation of childbirth. Abortion stood at the apex of all our nightmares and inhibitions about sex, and to tamper with it meant that the whole system could come tumbling down.[49]

170

> Once sex had been detached from pregnancy,
> women's liberation could construct its own ethics on
> the ash-heap of puritan morality. The single woman
> could no longer be terrorized by social ostracism; the
> married woman no longer forced into deeper subser-
> vience by an unwanted child.[50]

Sexual permissiveness and abortion go hand in hand. Sexual permissiveness necessitates the repeal of abortion laws to elim-inate undesired conceptions, and legal abortion makes sexual permissiveness more feasible.

Germaine Greer describes the feminist ideal of love, which presupposes sexual permissiveness.

> Our self-realizing person [the ideal] might claim to
> be capable of loving everybody because he cannot be
> threatened by anybody. Of course circumstances will
> limit the possibility of his loving everybody, but it
> would certainly be a fluke if such a character were
> to remain completely monogamous.[51]

> Her [the self-actualizing woman's] promiscuity re-
> sulting from her constant sexual desire, tenderness
> and interests in people, will not usually be differen-
> tiated from compulsive promiscuity or inability to
> say no, although it is fundamentally different.[52]

Greer's ideal of love, which expresses itself sexually, resembles Freud's oceanic feeling; it is directed towards everyone. In femi-nist theory, monogamous sex is unnatural; it is one of the bonds from which women need to be freed. The double standard (men can sow wild oats, have extramarital liaisons without the social condemnation a woman would incur) must be eradicated; and the way to do it, according to the feminists, is to give women the same sexual freedom men have. To experience sexual free-dom, women must have absolute assurance that they will not be required to bear children.

With such a view of sex, the destruction of marriage and the family cannot be far behind. Feminists do not criticize mar-riage because of its sexual restrictions alone. Feminists have generally accepted Engels' analysis of the origin of the family as the chief cause of oppression of women. Engels argued that the monogamous family "is based on the supremacy of the man, the express purpose being to produce children of undisputed paternity; such paternity is demanded because these children are later to come into their father's property as his natural heirs."[53] Monogamous marriage was not an expression of love; it was based on economic necessity. The ownership of private property, of which Engels obviously did not approve, created the need for natural heirs; consequently, a man had to insure his wife's fidelity. His fidelity to her was not essential, and so monogamous marriage put the woman at a disadvantage sexually. The individual family deprives the woman of her economic independence. Before the rise of the monogamous family, in communal homes, running the household and child care was a social duty. In the individual family, it is a private service. The wife cannot perform household duties and hold down a job (or one that pays well); as a result, she has no economic independence. Marriage then becomes an act of prostitution, in which women barter their bodies in return for economic security. Engels thought that only when the economic reasons for marriage were removed could there be the opportunity for genuine sexual love.

Feminists think that economic independence is necessary to maintain self-respect and sanity. Greer offers this analysis:

> Every wife must live with the knowledge that she has nothing else but home and family, while her house is ideally a base which her tired warrior-hunter can withdraw to and express his worst manners, his least amusing conversation, while he licks his wounds and is prepared by laundry and toilet and lunchbox for another sortie.
>
> Obviously any woman who thinks in the simplest terms of liberating herself to enjoy life and create expression for her own potential cannot accept such a role.[54]

What is the answer, according to Engels and the feminists?

> . . . the first condition for the liberation of the wife is to bring the whole female sex back into public industry, and that this in turn demands the abolition of the monogamous family as the economic unit of society.[55]

Note that Engels considers the return of women to the labor market a factor that contributes to the end of the monogamous family as the economic unit of society. The end of the family's economic function leads to its complete restructuring. When the means of production are transferred to common ownership, Engels predicts the communal "ownership" of children, and sexual freedom.

> With the transfer of the means of production into common ownership, the single family ceases to be the economic unit of society. Private housekeeping is transformed into a social industry. The care and education of the children becomes a public affair; society looks after all children alike, whether they are legitimate or not. This removes all the anxiety about the "consequences," which today is the most essential social—moral as well as economic—factor that prevents a girl from giving herself completely to the man she loves. Will not that suffice to bring about the gradual growth of unconstrained sexual intercourse and with it a more tolerant public opinion in regard to a maiden's honor and a woman's shame? And, finally, have we not seen that in the modern world monogamy and prostitution are indeed contradictions, but inseparable contradictions, poles of the same state of society? Can prostitution disappear without dragging monogamy with it into the abyss?[56]

According to the feminists, economic independence is necessary for women to be liberated. To obtain economic independence, they must enter the labor market. Feminists maintain that they want to give women a choice: to work or not. However, it is only an illusion of choice. To bring about the feminist ideal, all women must return to the labor market, as Engels prescribed. Simone de Beauvoir wrote the following to Betty Friedan in 1975:

> No woman should be authorized to stay at home to raise her children. Women should not have that choice, precisely because if there is such a choice, too many women will make that one. It is a way of forc-

173

> ing women in a certain direction. . . . In my opinion,
> as long as the family and the myth of the family and
> the myth of maternity and the maternal instinct are
> not destroyed, women will still be oppressed.[57]

Women's liberation claims to give women the option to work (an option women have already), but its real aim is to remove the option of homemaking and raising one's own children.

The Equal Rights Amendment will aid the feminist goal, getting women into the work force and destroying the monogamous family. How? For instance, ERA proponents have suggested that if the wife does not work outside the home, the husband should pay double social security, as if his wife were hired as housekeeper. This measure is supposed to give the role of homemaker more dignity. But it does not increase the woman's benefits; she already gets social security benefits from her husband's income. The effect of this proposal would be a decrease in net family income, which would probably force some women into the labor market.

ERA would also remove the husband's legal obligation to support his wife and children, an obligation based on the fact that women bear children. The removal of this "sexist" law will eliminate the legal support for the right of the woman to stay at home and take care of her own children. Rather than giving women the option of working or not, ERA subtly undermines the role of homemaker and forces women into the labor market. Discarding the wife's right to support also makes it easier for husbands to leave their families (no more alimony), and so ERA works against the institution of the family.

Feminists also see ERA as a means of getting the woman's right to abortion into the Constitution. When asked about the connection between ERA and abortion, Betty Friedan answered that future Supreme Courts could not be trusted to follow the 1973 decision on abortion: "That's the reason we need ERA."[58] The Supreme Court discovered the woman's supposed right to abortion in the 14th Amendment; for a hundred years, however, no one knew that this "right" was there. The states that ratified the amendment certainly did not. Consequently, feminists cannot rely on future Supreme Courts to uphold the right to abortion based on the 14th Amendment; that is one reason they need ERA.

ERA also means government child care. Child care outside the home is not in itself undesirable. However, to advocate government funding of child care so that mothers can be free to fulfill professional, educational, or personal goals, as the Ohio Task Force for the Implementation of the Equal Rights Amendment phrases it, implies that *parents* are not responsible for the care of their own children. It gives that responsibility to the government. In addition, one feminist states, "Our demand for collective public child care is throwing into question the private family ownership of children."[59] Common "ownership" of children means the end of the family.

An opponent of women's liberation summarizes:

> The movement literature paints marriage as slavery, the home as a prison, the husband as the oppressor, family as an anachronism no longer relevant to woman's happiness, and children as the daily drudgery from which the modern woman must be freed in order to pursue more fulfilling careers.[60]

And concerning ERA:

> ERA will prevent us forever from making reasonable differences between men and women based on factual differences in child-bearing and physical strength. ERA will force upon us the rigid, unisex, gender-free mandate demanded by the women's liberation movement, and it will transfer the power to apply this mandate to the federal government and the federal courts, where average citizens have no control.[61]

Feminists advocate a total revolution, of which abortion on demand is an integral part. The revolution involves complete sexual freedom, including lesbianism, the destruction of monogamous marriage and the family, government child care, the end of occupation housewife and/or mother, and the obliteration of all distinctions between men and women, except physical differences. When we consider the issue of abortion, we should not consider it in isolation; it is a part of a cluster of ideas. When we consider whether or not we favor the right to abortion, we must consider whether or not we favor the accompanying cultural changes.

We must also ask if the feminist analysis of the situation is correct. Is the family a part of capitalism's system of exploitation? No, the family existed before capitalism. Rather than creating the family, capitalism may be responsible for whittling the family down to its bare nucleus. The family produces a very different mentality from that of laissez-faire capitalism: mutuality as opposed to extreme individualism.

> The strength of the traditional family in resisting the capitalist mentality has always been its firm belief in mutuality, complementarity, and natural obligations that exist independently of benefits received.[62]

The family is also a bulwark of resistance against totalitarianism, and so protects individual rights and freedoms. Erich Fromm, Bruno Bettelheim, and Theodor Adorno have studied which personality type is most susceptible to mass movements and authoritarian ideologies. It is the uprooted, homeless, wandering urbanite, whom liberationists have held up as models of liberation.[63] Remember, the feminists' proposals would give the federal government more control over our lives (consider what universal child care could mean in terms of mass indoctrination). Is not increasing governmental control drawing us toward a totalitarian state? Erich Fromm warns in *Escape from Freedom:*

> Modern man . . . has become free from the external bonds that would prevent him from doing and thinking as he sees fit. He would be free to act according to his own will, if he knew what he wanted, thought, and felt. But he does not know. He conforms to anonymous authorities and adopts a self that is not his. . . . In spite of a veneer of optimism and initiative, modern man is overcome by a profound feeling of powerlessness . . . the despair of the human automaton is fertile soil for the political purposes of fascism.[64]

176

The feminists' hostility toward the family may have another cause. Feminists may oppose the family because the family fosters mutuality rather than egotism. A family, in the true sense of the word, works together for the benefit of all; sharing and consideration of the rights of others are learned in the family. Feminists may claim to deplore capitalism's emphasis on the individual ego and may mention community as a goal. Yet their own emphasis is exclusively on *individual* fulfillment and *individual* economic independence. Self-sacrifice, a quality implied in the family's teaching of mutuality, is incomprehensible to the feminist. Greer illustrates this incomprehension in her discussion of love. The ideal is "the principle of love that is reaffirmed in the relationship of the narcissistic self to the world of which it is a part."[65]

> I have talked of love as an assertion of confidence in the self, an extension of narcissism to include one's own kind, variously considered. And yet we are told, "Greater love hath no man than he lay down his life for his friend." . . . That understanding of love was that it was the negation by abnegation of the self, the forgetfulness of the self in humility, patience, and self-denial. The essential egotism of the practice was apparent to many of us in the demeanor of the most pious girls, for the aim of the exercise was ultimately to earn grace in the eyes of the Lord . . .[66]

> The ideal of altruism is possibly a high one, but it is unfortunately chimeric. We cannot be liberated from ourselves, and we cannot act in defiance of our own motivations, unless we are mother ducks and act as instinctive creatures, servants of the species. We, the children who were on the receiving end, knew that our mothers' self-sacrifice existed mostly in their minds. . . . We could see that our mothers blackmailed us with self-sacrifice . . .[67]

Greer considers self-sacrifice impossible; every act has a selfish motive. Undoubtedly, many altruistic actions have selfish motives, but that does not mean that all do or that the goal of self-sacrifice is bad. Notice that Greer's way does not promise real liberation; she advocates giving in to self, to selfish motivations.

Egotism is not an attractive banner, so Greer attempts to redefine it.

> If altruism is chimeric, it does not follow that all love behavior is basically egotistical. The narcissism that I pointed to as the basis for love is not a phenomenon of the ego, which is only the conscious, self-conscious part of the personality, but a function of the whole personality. [How does the involvement of the whole personality, as opposed to the ego, defend Greer's ideal of love against the accusation of selfishness?] Egotism in love is not the love of one for another of its own kind, but the assumption of a unity existing between two people which must be enforced and protected against all attempts to socialize it. If a person loves only one other person, and is indifferent to the rest of his fellow men, his love is not love but a symbiotic attachment, or an enlarged egotism.[68]

According to Greer, it is selfish to love only one person (monogamous marriage). This notion carries over into the mother-child relation. "For the really liberated woman, the love of the mother for her child is antisocial because it differentiates that child from all other children. . . . The theory behind this is that we would love humanity the more if we ceased to love certain individuals so intensely."[69] The opposite is really the case; we love others by the extension of familial love (e.g., "the brotherhood of man" or the feminist slogan "sisterhood is powerful").

> In another women's lib utopia, "adult-child relationships would develop just as do the best relationships today; some adults might prefer certain children over others, just as some children might prefer certain adults over others"! This is supposed to be an ideal egalitarian community, but there is nothing as inegalitarian as popularity. Although families may be "unequal," each child has a particular mother and father who love it because it is their own, even if the child next door is cleverer, prettier and more

appealing. In a communal environment with no fixed ties, the most attractive children are likely to get all the adult affection and attention, while the unattractive child enjoys his inalienable human "right" to loneliness and neglect.[70]

The family provides a model for unconditional love; to give love unconditionally implies self-sacrifice, self-denial, acceptance of and love for others no matter what they do. On the other hand, the feminist views each person as a rootless individual, whose chief aim is self-fulfillment; she has no commitments to or dependence on any one else. Her relations with others change at her convenience, when she desires. Each woman is to have such confidence in herself that these changes will cause no psychological or emotional damage. The assessment by Arianna Stassinopoulos is accurate: "The ideal which is to replace altruism is the autonomous, calculated search for individual self-realization—relationships are seen simply as an aspect of the individual's egocentric fixation."[71] The feminists always choose personal freedom at the expense of caring for others.

This choice is perfectly exemplified by the feminists' attitude towards abortion. The feminists assert the individual's right to control her own body; her own selfish concerns and welfare become the only standard for her behavior. Abortion is the epitome of autonomy.

The feminists' attitude towards children also reveals their self-centered orientation. Children's liberation has a place within the feminist movement. But what children's liberation really means is to abandon the children so that the parents can be free, so that the parents will not have to give up anything or defer to the needs of the young and vulnerable.

> The specific indifference to children of some feminists bears an unpleasant resemblance to society's general indifference to the future . . .[72]

The lack of concern for children may parallel the unwillingness to conserve energy for the sake of future generations; both evidence a self-indulgent attitude.

Feminism, especially as it is expressed by Betty Friedan, promotes the illusion that work is the answer to women's fulfillment. It is true that many women feel frustrated at being housewives. They are bored. But feminist ideology fails to confront the cold, hard facts that most jobs are boring and that working as well as marriage or motherhood can be a form of slavery. Women ought to have the right to work and women should receive equal pay for equal work, writes Benjamin Barber:

> But to treat work as a possible solution to the dilemmas of self-realization in a world where neither productivity nor reproductivity can any longer by themselves define our identities is to forget the liberationist's point of departure.[73]

Feminists believe that their revolution is necessary for the welfare of women and of society as a whole. They believe the end justifies their irresponsibility and overstatements ("marriage is the ultimate act of prostitution"). They genuinely believe they know what is best. But do they?

History, though perhaps not an infallible guide, suggests that the feminist vision will not work. In Russia, Engels' principles for the equalization of the sexes were put into practice in the 1920s and early 1930s. Easy abortion, open marriage, easy divorce, sexual freedom, devaluation of the family, elimination of sex roles, communal living, and universal child care by the state were practiced. The results were disastrous, as Amaury de Riencourt describes in *Sex and Power in History*:

> The collapse of family solidarity resulted in the mushrooming of juvenile delinquency on a staggering scale, and far from raising the status of woman, the revolution proved to be utterly demoralizing. Rather than freeing woman, it had freed *man* from sexual restraints and domestic responsibility. . . . In fact, the new Soviet female was as sexually oppressed as she had never been before . . .[74]

Nor has the liberation of women in Red China or the Israeli *kibbutz* raised the status of women in politics or the professions. ". . . the history of unisex revolution teaches that in the long run women are freed from homes and children largely to do low-paying manual work dictated by the state."[75]

180

Sweden may be suggested as a successful example of feminist ideals in operation, but in Sweden:

> The freedom of the individual was sacrificed to the interests of the total state, which in exchange removed all traditional morality from its laws and encouraged all of the conditions that seem to be emerging as progressive wisdom in the United States, such as contractual marriage, easy divorce, easy abortion, unmarried cohabitation, illegitimacy . . . sex education, pornography, and universal day-care services. In addition, the state sided with the children against their elders in order to mold them to the official values. The mass media became organs of advocacy, working to help form the opinions desirable to the regime. The attitudes of the people were molded by squads of "experts."[76]

Some critics of feminism, "naturalists" such as George Gilder and Steven Goldberg, consider feminism a form of sexual suicide and the end of society.

> When a society deliberately affirms these failures— contemplates legislation of homosexual marriage, celebrates the women who denounce the family, and indulges pornography as a manifestation of sexual health and a release from repression—the culture is promoting a form of erotic suicide. For it is destroying the cultural preconditions of profound love and sexuality: the durable heterosexual relationships necessary to a community of emotional investments and continuities in which children can find a secure place.[77]

The family is the institution through which we can survive the current social crisis, but the naturalists carry this idea further. To uphold the family, the woman must remain mother. She must never compete with men. For these opponents of feminism, anatomy is destiny; and for women to be happy, they should not rebel against their own natures. To appease women, the naturalists also assure us that maternity is power—women have the *real* advantage.

181

The idea that the father is inherently equal to the mother within the family, or that he will necessarily be inclined to remain within it, is nonsense. In one way or another, the man must be made equal by society.[78]

... the men counterbalance female sexual superiority by playing a crucial role as provider and achiever. ...

If women become equal in terms of money and achievement, there is only one way equality between the sexes can be maintained in a modern society. Women must be reduced to sexual parity. They must relinquish their sexual superiority, psychologically disconnect their wombs, and adopt the short-circuited copulatory sexuality of the males. Women must renounce all the larger procreative dimensions of their sexual impulse.[79]

Women, under this scheme, are relegated to reproduction; as compensation for being unable to bear children, men produce and achieve—in business, art, science, and so on. Each sex is to stay in its own area. If the balance is upset, the end of society is imminent. In their veneration for the family, the naturalists fail to recognize that men have at times used the family to oppress women. Even when the necessity for the woman to stay at home decreased (something the naturalists seem unaware of), the man, in the guise of protecting the woman, kept her there in an effort to guard his own rights. The naturalists do not admit that there is a problem for women unless it be feminism. They fail to see that women, as human beings, have intellectual and spiritual needs that are not met by maternity.

Too often the choice offered to women is "the choice of total subservience to men, children, and their own wombs [the naturalist alternative], or total liberation from everything that defines them as women [the women's lib alternative]."[80] Are these the only choices?

How do we know what is best for society, for women? History makes suggestions, but is there a way to know with certainty? Another approach to the same question is to ask: On what basis do we make laws? This question brings us back to the issue of abortion. In the case of abortion, abortionists assume there is no absolute moral standard; the decision is to be made subjectively—it is up to the woman. This is a situation ethics. It is not new. What happens when subjectivity replaces an absolute moral standard as the basis for law? Near the end of his discerning analysis of civilization, Francis Schaeffer writes:

> Man has failed to build only from himself autonomously and to find a solid basis in nature for law, and we are left today with Oliver Wendell Holmes's "experience" and Frederick Moore Vinson's statement that nothing is more certain in modern society than that there are no absolutes. Law has only a variable content. Much modern law is not even based on precedent; that is, it does not necessarily hold fast to a continuity with the legal decisions of the past. Thus, within a wide range, the Constitution of the United States can be made to say what the courts of the present want it to say—based on a court's decision as to what the court feels is sociologically helpful at the moment . . . but once the door is opened, anything can become law and the arbitrary judgments of men are king. Law is now freewheeling, and the courts not only interpret the laws which legislators have made, but make law. *Lex Rex* has become *Rex Lex*. Arbitrary judgment concerning current sociological good is *king.*[81]

Schaeffer warns, *"If there are no absolutes by which to judge society, then society is absolute. . . .* Arbitrary absolutes can be handed down and there is no absolute by which to judge them."[82] One man, an elite, or the majority vote can determine what is legal or "right." Subjectivity in law (and morality), as the feminists advocate, produces unrestrained freedom—anarchy—and finally results in authoritarianism. We can see that the feminists are headed in this direction because of their increasing dependence on government regulation.

Schaeffer concludes that there is only one thing that can insure the dignity of the individual and give him the possibility of meaningful freedom without anarchy: God's revelation in the Bible. God's Word is the moral absolute, by which all laws and society can be judged; and God's Word certifies what works, what behavior and structures enable men and women to retain their humanity. Feminism and "naturalism" are to be judged by biblical standards. Both fall short, as a brief comparison illustrates.

In contrast to feminism, the Bible upholds monogamous marriage. Sex belongs only in marriage. Sex belongs only in marriage because it is an act that forms a permanent bond between a man and a woman (I Corinthians 6:16). Sex should express commitment, faithfulness, and love. But contrary to some naturalist notions, the Bible does not indicate that the *only* purpose of sex is reproduction (Song of Solomon; Proverbs 5:18), and women are not to be defined solely as mothers (Luke 11:27–28). Marital sex reflects the mutuality of husband and wife; this idea resembles feminist ideals more than those of the naturalist. In I Corinthians 7:2–5, Paul teaches that sexual intercourse may be initiated by either husband or wife; in sexual matters, the husband's body belongs to his wife, and hers belongs to him.

According to the Bible, men and women in general are dependent on one another, and the purpose of this dependence is to point to our dependence on God (I Corinthians 11:11–12). The woman's bearing children is a demonstration of the man's dependence on her (for existence), not a sign of servitude. The feminists seek to free themselves from any reliance on men; this desire for autonomy signifies their rebellion against God.

The Bible does not support the strict role differentiation (the husband works; the wife stays at home) often espoused by naturalists. In Genesis, both the man and the woman are told to subdue the earth (work) and reproduce. Both mother and father are to discipline and teach their children (Proverbs 1:8; Ephesians 6:4), which are a blessing from the Lord (Psalm 127: 3–5). Children are not the special domain of women. In Proverbs 31:10ff., the ideal wife works outside as well as in the home. She buys land and farms it (v. 16); she makes garments and sells them to merchants (v. 24). In Acts, we meet Lydia, a business woman, and Priscilla, who was a tentmaker. Yet the career orientation that neglects all other things is not warranted either, for women or men. Although women are not confined to the home and although women should have a role in subduing the earth, women (and men, I Timothy 3:4, 12) are not to neglect home or family. Paul instructs the older women to teach the younger women to love their husbands and children, to be sensible, chaste, home workers, kind and submissive to their own husbands (Titus 2:4–5).

184

Three scriptural principles regarding male-female relations do not concur with either feminist or naturalist dogma. (1) Both men and women are created in God's image. In other words, men and women are equal in being, as persons. The naturalists fail to do full justice to this principle. (2) Women are to submit themselves to men in two areas, wives to their own husbands, and women to the elders in the Church. This submission can be termed functional or economic subordination. It is the voluntary submission of one equal to another. Feminists deny this principle. (3) Husband and wife are one flesh (sexual intercourse initiates and reaffirms this union), and believers in the Church form one body. The union of husband and wife is the foundation of love in marriage; because they are one, the husband is not to abuse his position of authority. To abuse his wife would be the same as abusing himself. He is to care for and cherish his wife as himself.

The feminists may protest, with justification, that these three principles are not working well at present. Men do not acknowledge women as equal persons; men treat women as sex objects, mindless bodies, inferiors, children, with patronage and condescension. Husbands do not treat their wives with love and consideration. And wives do not submit to their husbands. Why should they? That would only make the situation worse.

The Bible has an explanation for the current state of affairs. Sin not only disrupts one's relation with God; it disrupts interpersonal relations. As a result of the Fall (Genesis 3), the woman desires to control her husband. She rejects God's authority structure in marriage. The husband, therefore, has to fight for his headship. To undergird his authority, he resorts to denying the personhood of his wife. He attempts to belittle her in order to protect himself and his rights. The feminists' answer to this sin-ridden situation is to perpetuate and institutionalize the sinful tendencies of the Fall—the woman's rejection and usurpation of her husband's headship.

The biblical solution is: Wives, submit yourselves to your husbands; and husbands, love your wives. When each obeys the command addressed to him or her, the proper order for marriage is resumed. When wives acknowledge their husbands' headship, husbands no longer have to fight for it by demeaning and mistreating their wives. When husbands love their wives, wives no longer have to fight for their own personhood. Then the battle of the sexes would end.

On the most fundamental level, the war between the sexes can be ended only when the power of sin is destroyed in men and women. Christ has accomplished this on the cross by paying the penalty for sin on behalf of humanity. All those who believe in him are freed from sin's dominion. A right relation with God through Christ is the foundation for having the right relations with others.

The Bible also provides the answer to personal fulfillment. Friedan suggests that meaningful work is the answer; others have suggested material possessions, education or knowledge, art, love, family. But none of these provides lasting satisfaction, and all of them are only shadows that point to the real thing. The answer is a relation with God through Jesus Christ. Pascal called this need a God-shaped vacuum.

Fulfillment of self paradoxically means denial of self. Jesus said (Matthew 16:24–25):

> If any man would come after me, let him deny himself and take up his cross and follow me. For whoever would save his life will lose it, and whoever loses his life for my sake will find it.

Greer is wrong; escape from selfishness and egotism is possible. The One who commands it is the One who practiced perfect (altruistic) love, who gave up His life for sinners, and the One who commands it is the One who enables His followers to obey this command and to love. The pursuit of personal fulfillment is vain, but if one gives one's life to Christ, if one puts Christ's kingdom first, before one's own desires, then one will find enduring joy and peace.

One of the most important values taught in the Bible is the value of individual human life. Each person is made in God's image and therefore deserves respect and has dignity. The fact that each human life is intrinsically worthwhile, regardless of a person's achievements, genetic sufficiency, or capability for independent life or "meaningful" life, attests to the immorality of abortion.

Although the feminist solution to the woman's problem is mistaken, feminists are sincerely concerned about women and have accomplished some reforms important to the welfare of women. Feminists have improved the lot of victims of rape and have brought wife-beating to public attention. They have tried to show compassion to the woman who has become pregnant in difficult circumstances. Too often, pro-life advocates forget the plight of the expectant mother in their defense of the fetus' right to live. Pro-lifers talk of the mother's responsibility for her own situation without realizing that she needs help to face her responsibilities. The biblical command is to show compassion. Pro-life advocates must understand for themselves and point out to others that it is not true compassion to allow the expectant mother to take a human life to ease her situation, no matter how desperate it may seem. Those who oppose abortion must propose programs to help women who feel that abortion is the only answer to their problem. As mentioned before, there should be counseling clinics to give emotional support and to help the woman adjust to having a child. The woman should be encouraged to give up her baby for adoption or to a foster home if she is unable to care for him herself. Maternity leave and child care are two other possible aids.

Measures to help the woman with the "problem" pregnancy are not the final answer. The answer is to prevent women from having "problem" pregnancies. Part of the solution is accurate and available information about contraception. But a more important and basic aspect of the solution is a change in attitudes and values, a return to "traditional" morality—biblical morality. Sexual intercourse must be put back into its proper context, marriage. In addition, persons need to be reeducated to accept responsibility for their own actions, that is, to acknowledge that sexual intercourse, even with contraception, may result in pregnancy; therefore, if one engages in sex, he or she must be willing to accept the responsibility for a child. Although this responsibility should be accepted, it is not a burden because of the effectiveness of contraceptive devices when properly used. Another value that needs reaffirmation is that children are a gift from God. The unplanned conception is not a curse but a blessing.

Abortion from the feminist standpoint is based on the woman's right to control her own body. This right enables her to achieve equality with the man (she can now escape childbearing, a handicap in the pursuit of a career or fulfillment) and independence of the man (economically). The most serious objection to the feminists' rationale for abortion is that it avoids the reality of the fetus; it denies that the fetus is a separate human life with rights of his own. The woman's right to control her own body implies a total social revolution—complete sexual freedom, the end of monogamous marriage and the family, and government child care. This "right" bespeaks a self-centered mentality, which the feminists claim is good. Women's liberation promises new freedoms to women, freedom from motherhood, from men, from morality, from responsibilities, freedom to be an individual; but the price of these "freedoms" is bondage to self on a personal level and increased governmental control on a social level. The feminists' argument for abortion is inadequate on both levels. On the personal, it promotes self-centeredness to the point of destroying another human life; on the social, it promises complete individual freedom, which has historically resulted in loss of individuality and loss of freedom.

Notes

1. Lawrence Lader, *Abortion II: Making the Revolution* (Boston: Beacon Press, 1973), p. 36.

2. *Ibid.,* p. 39.

3. Lucina Cisler, "Unfinished Business: Birth Control and Women's Liberation," in Robin Morgan, ed., *Sisterhood is Powerful* (New York: Vintage, 1970), pp. 274–75.

4. *Ibid.,* p. 274.

5. Alice S. Rossi, ed., *The Feminist Papers: From Adams to de Beauvoir* (New York: Columbia University Press, 1973), p. 517.

6. Betty Friedan, "Our Revolution is Unique," in Mary Lou Thompson, ed., *Voices of the New Feminism* (Boston: Beacon Press, 1970), p. 34.

7. Cisler, "Unfinished Business," p. 309.

8. Donald DeMarco, *Abortion in Perspective: the Rose Palace or the Fiery Dragon?* (Cincinnati: Hiltz & Hayes, 1974), pp. 166–67.

9. C. Everett Koop, M.D., *The Right to Live, The Right to Die* (Wheaton, Ill.: Tyndale House, 1976), p. 56.

10. Lader, *Abortion II,* p. 21.

11. Friedan, "Our Revolution Is Unique," pp. 34–35.

12. Lader, *Abortion II,* p. xi.

13. *Ibid.,* p. ix.

14. Margaret Sanger, "Birth Control: A Parents' Problem or Woman's," in Rossi, ed., *Feminist Papers,* p. 533.

15. Lader, *Abortion II,* p. 20.

16. Cisler, "Unfinished Business," p. 299.

17. Lader, *Abortion II,* p. xi.

18. *Ibid.,* p. 20.

19. Garrett Hardin, "The History and Future of Birth Control," *Perspectives in Biology and Medicine,* 10:1 (1966), quoted by Cisler, "Unfinished Business," p. 299.

20. James H. Olthuis, *I Pledge You My Troth: A Christian View of Marriage, Family, Friendship* (New York: Harper & Row, 1975), p. 77.

21. Garrett Hardin, "Abortion—Or Compulsory Pregnancy?" *Journal of Marriage and the Family,* 30 (1968), p. 248.

22. Peter Steinfels, "Women and the 'Feminist Ethic'—II," *Commonweal,* March 3, 1972, p. 518.

23. DeMarco, *Abortion in Perspective,* p. 48.

24. Alfred Kotasek, "Artificial Termination of Pregnancy in Czechoslovakia," *International Journal of Gynecology and Obstetrics,* 9:3 (1971), quoted in DeMarco, *Abortion in Perspective,* p. 49.

25. DeMarco, *Abortion in Perspective,* p. 118.

26. Cisler, "Unfinished Business," p. 304; Lader, *Abortion II,* p. 21.

27. Robert M. Byrn, "Goodbye to the Judeo-Christian Era in Law," *America,* June 2, 1973, p. 512.

28. Mary Daly, "Abortion and Sexual Caste," *Commonweal,* February 4, 1972, pp. 415–18.

29. Cisler, "Unfinished Business," p. 301.

30. Beverly Jones, "The Dynamics of Marriage and Motherhood," in Morgan, ed., *Sisterhood Is Powerful,* p. 54.

31. Lader, *Abortion II,* pp. 23–24.

32. DeMarco, *Abortion in Perspective,* p. 109.

33. *Ibid.,* p. 26.

34. *Ibid.,* pp. 163–64.

35. Quoted *ibid.,* p. 164.

36. Hardin, "Compulsory Pregnancy?" pp. 250–51.

37. Lader, *Abortion II,* p. 21.

38. *Ibid.,* p. 21.

39. *Ibid.,* p. 35.

40. *Ibid.,* p. 172.

41. DeMarco, *Abortion in Perspective,* p. 95.

42. Lader, *Abortion II,* p. 34.

43. Daly, "Abortion and Sexual Caste," pp. 417–18.

44. Cisler, "Unfinished Business," p. 309.

45. Phyllis Chesler, *Women and Madness* (Garden City, N.Y.: Doubleday, 1972), p. 299.

46. Phyllis Schlafly, *The Power of the Positive Woman* (New Rochelle, N.Y.: Arlington House, 1977), p. 12.

47. Betty Friedan, *The Feminine Mystique* (New York: Dell, 1974), p. 370.

48. Kate Millett, *Sexual Politics* (Garden City, N. Y.: Doubleday, 1970), p. 62.

49. Lader, *Abortion II,* p. viii.

50. *Ibid.,* p. 212.

51. Germaine Greer, *The Female Eunuch* (New York: Bantam Books, 1971), p. 152.

52. *Ibid.,* p. 153.

53. Friedrich Engels, "The Origin of the Family," in Rossi, ed., *The Feminist Papers,* p. 481.

54. Greer, *Female Eunuch,* pp. 247–48.

55. Engels, "Origin of the Family," p. 487.

56. *Ibid.,* pp. 488–89.

57. Quoted in Jim and Andrea Fordham, *The Assault on the Sexes* (New Rochelle: Arlington House, 1977), pp. 437–38.

58. Betty Friedan, speaking on "Town Meeting of the Air," May 14, 1975, quoted in Schlafly, *Power of the Positive Woman,* p. 88.

59. Roxanne Dunbar, "Female Liberation as the Basis for Social Revolution," in Thompson, ed., *Voices,* p. 53.

60. Schlafly, *Positive Woman,* p. 46.

61. Ibid., p. 133.

62. Benjamin R. Barber, *Liberating Feminism* (New York: Dell, 1976), pp. 61–62.

63. *Ibid.,* p. 64.

64. *Ibid.,* pp. 64–65.

65. Quoted *ibid.,* p. 65.

66. Greer, *Female Eunuch,* p. 154.

67. *Ibid.,* p. 156.

68. *Ibid.,* p. 157.

69. Ibid., p. 160.

70. Arianna Stassinopoulos, *The Female Woman* (New York: Random House, 1973), pp. 61–62.

71. Ibid., p. 65. Quotes Shulamith Firestone, *The Dialectics of Sex: The Case for Feminist Revolution* (London: Jonathan Cape, 1971), p. 217.

72. Stassinopoulos, *Female Woman,* p. 6.

73. Barber, *Liberating Feminism,* p. 54.

74. Quoted in Fordham, *Assault,* p. 439.

75. Fordham, *Assault,* pp. 442–43.

76. *Ibid.,* pp. 441–42.

77. George F. Gilder, *Sexual Suicide* (New York: Quadrangle, 1973), p. 5.

78. *Ibid.,* p. 14.

79. *Ibid.,* p. 15.

80. Barber, *Liberating Feminism,* p. xv.

81. Francis A. Schaeffer, *How Should We Then Live?: The Rise and Decline of Western Thought and Culture* (Old Tappan, N.J.: Fleming H. Revell, 1976), p. 218.

82. *Ibid.,* p. 224.

About the Authors

C. EVERETT KOOP received his B.A. from Dartmouth and his M.D. from Cornell Medical College. He is surgeon-in-chief of the Children's Hospital of Pennsylvania and professor of pediatrics and pediatric surgery at the School of Medicine, the University of Pennsylvania. He is the author of *The Right to Live, the Right to Die* and *Visible and Palpable Lesions in Children.* Dr. Koop is also the editor-in-chief of the *Journal of Pediatric Surgery.*

RICHARD L. GANZ was born in New York City and went to Hunter College of the City University of New York, where he received his B.A. in psychology. He received his M.A. and Ph.D. in clinical psychology from Wayne State University. He has taught at both Wayne State University and Syracuse University. Dr. Ganz has been on the staff of the Syracuse Veterans Administration Hospital and the clinical faculty of the department of psychiatry of the Upstate Medical Center. In 1978 he completed work for the M. Div. at Westminster Theological Seminary. He serves on the staff of the Christian Counseling and Educational Foundation with Dr. Jay E. Adams.

JOHN M. FRAME received his B.A. in philosophy from Princeton University, his M.A. and M. Phil. in religious studies from Yale. He is currently a candidate for the Ph.D. in philosophy (Yale) and an associate professor of systematic theology at Westminster Theological Seminary. He is the author of *Abor-*

tion and Christian Assumptions and *The Amsterdam Philosophy: A Preliminary Critique.* His papers "God and Biblical Language" and "Scripture Speaks for Itself" appeared in *God's Inerrant Word.*

JEREMY C. JACKSON was born in Cheshire, England, and received his B.A. from Cambridge University and his Ph.D. in history from the University of Pennsylvania. He spent three years working with Dr. Francis Schaeffer at L'Abri in Switzerland, and has taught at William and Mary College and Syracuse University. He has recently been a historical consultant to Dr. Schaeffer while completing a volume on church history.

HAROLD O.J. BROWN received his B.A., B.D., Th.M., and Ph.D. degrees from Harvard University. He is the author of four books: *The Protest of a Troubled Protestant, Christianity and the Class Struggle, The Reconstruction of the Republic,* and *Death before Birth* (on abortion). From 1972 to 1974 he was associate editor of *Christianity Today.* Now a professor of theology at Trinity Evangelical Divinity School, he is editor of the *Human Life Review* and chairman of the Christian Action Council.

PAUL D. FEINBERG is associate professor and chairman of the division of philosophy of religion at Trinity Evangelical Divinity School in Deerfield, Illinois.

Dr. Feinberg received his B.A. in history from the University of California, Los Angeles. He was granted his B.D. and Th.M. degrees at Talbot Theological Seminary in La Mirada, California, followed by the Th.D. in systematic theology from Dallas Theological Seminary. Dr. Feinberg took an M.A. in philosophy at Roosevelt University in Chicago, Illinois, and is currently a candidate for the Ph.D. degree in philosophy at the University of Chicago.

Besides Trinity Evangelical Divinity School, Dr. Feinberg has served the faculties of Moody Bible Institute and Trinity College. He has also been a field evangelist for the American Board of Missions to the Jews, Inc.

SUSAN T. FOH received a B.A. in English from Wellesley College and a master of arts in religion from Westminster Theological Seminary, where she later worked for three years as assistant librarian. Mrs. Foh is currently working on a book about women and the Bible.

Index